CROCK·POT®
EXPRESS CROCK
MULTI-COOKER

FIX IT
FAST
— OR —
SLOW

pil

Publications International, Ltd.

Pictured on the front cover: Barbecue Ribs *(page 162)*.

Pictured on the back cover *(clockwise from top left):* Hot Beef Sandwiches au Jus *(page 142)*, Vegetable Egg Nests *(page 112)*, Chicken Cacciatore *(page 104)*, Denver Egg Bowls *(page 108)*, Weeknight Beef Stew *(page 88)*, Brownie Bottoms *(page 242)*, German Potato Salad *(page 194)*, Boneless Pork Roast with Garlic *(page 150)* and Spicy Chicken Chili *(page 72)*.

Note: The recipes in this book are for use in the Crock-Pot® Express Crock Multi-Cooker. While today's multi-cookers are built with safety features, you MUST follow the instructions which come with your multi-cooker. IF YOU DO NOT FOLLOW THE SAFETY INSTRUCTIONS CAREFULLY, INJURY OR DAMAGE MAY RESULT.

CONTENTS

EXPRESS CROCK MULTI-COOKER 101

THE FAST PRESSURE COOKER WITH SLOW COOKER CONVENIENCE

In today's fast-paced world, you need a Multi-Cooker that can keep up with your lifestyle. Let the **CROCK-POT®** brand handle the pressure of mealtime with the **CROCK-POT®** Express Crock Multi-Cooker. Express Crock can cook meals up to 70% faster than traditional cooking, so you can spend less time in the kitchen and more time with your family.

When you're in a hurry, choose from 8 preset pressurized settings for the same taste you love in less time. Of course, if you're not ready to eat now, you can choose the SLOW COOK setting—just set the cook time and come back later to a delicious, hot dish that's ready to eat when you are.

Easily prepare any recipe in this cookbook—whether it's slow cooked, steamed, sautéed or pressure cooked—using one convenient appliance. The nonstick cooking pot resists stuck-on food and is dishwasher safe, making clean-up a breeze.

For more than 45 years, the **CROCK-POT®** brand has been your trusted brand for cooking convenience. The **CROCK-POT®** brand is a leader in one-pot cooking, and this Express Crock cooking collection is the perfect addition to your kitchen.

WHAT EXACTLY IS A PRESSURE COOKER?

It's a simple concept: Liquid is heated in a heavy pot with a lid that locks and forms an airtight seal. Since the steam from the hot liquid is trapped inside and can't evaporate, the pressure increases and raises the boiling point of the contents in the pot, and these items cook faster at a higher temperature. In general, pressure cooking can reduce cooking time to about one third of the time used in conventional cooking methods—and typically the time spent on pressure cooking is hands off. (There's no peeking or stirring when food is being cooked under pressure.)

EXPRESS CROCK COMPONENTS

Before beginning to cook, make sure you're familiar with the basic parts of the **CROCK-POT®** Express Crock Multi-Cooker. Always refer to your manual for more details and to answer questions about your specific model.

The **heating base** is where the electrical components are housed. It should never be immersed in water. To clean, simply unplug the unit, wipe it with a damp cloth and dry it immediately.

The **cooking pot** holds the food and fits snugly into the heating base. It has a nonstick coating and is removable. Inside the cooking pot are markings to guide the fill level. The ⅓, ½ and ⅔ markings are handy guides to use in the recipes.

The **control panel** typically shows a time that indicates where the multi-cooker is in a particular function. The time counts down to zero from the number of minutes that were programmed. (When pressure cooking, the timing begins once the machine reaches pressure.)

The **steam release** valve is on top of the lid and is used to seal the pot or release steam. To seal the pot, move the valve to the sealing or locked position; to release pressure, move the valve to the venting or open position. This valve can pop off to clean, and to make sure nothing is blocking it.

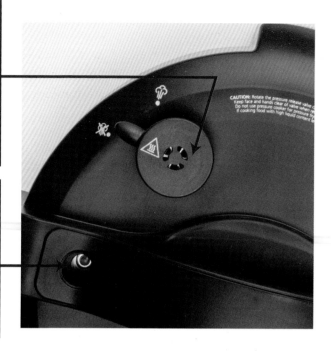

The **bobber valve** controls the amount of pressure inside the pressure cooker and indicates when pressure cooking is taking place—the valve rises once the contents of the pot reach working pressure; it drops down when all the pressure has been released after cooking.

The **steam release valve cover** is a small stainless steel cage found on the inside of the lid that prevents the pressure cooker from clogging. It can be removed for cleaning.

The **gasket fixing ring** underneath the lid helps create a tight seal to facilitate pressure cooking. The sealing ring has a tendency to absorb strong odors from cooking (particularly from acidic ingredients); washing it regularly with warm soapy water will help these odors dissipate, as will storing your pressure cooker with the lid ring side up. If you cook both sweet and savory dishes frequently, you may want to purchase an extra sealing ring (so the scent of curry or pot roast doesn't affect your rice pudding or custard). Make sure to inspect the ring before cooking—if it has any splits or cracks, it will not work properly and should be replaced.

PRESSURE COOKING BASICS

Every recipe is slightly different, but most include these basic steps. Read through the entire recipe before beginning to cook so you'll know what ingredients to add and when to add them, which pressure cooking function to use, the cooking time and the release method.

1. BROWN/SAUTÉ: Many recipes call for sautéing vegetables or browning meat at the beginning of a recipe to add flavor. (Be sure to leave the lid off in this step.)

2. Add the ingredients as the recipe directs and secure the lid, making sure it is properly locked according to the instruction manual. Turn the pressure release valve to the "Seal" (closed) position.

3. Choose from the pressure cooking functions (STEAM, MEAT/STEW, BEANS/CHILI, RICE/RISOTTO, POULTRY, DESSERT, SOUP or MULTIGRAIN). Set pressure to HIGH or LOW and set the cooking time. Press START/STOP.

4. Once the pressure cooking is complete, use the pressure release method directed by the recipe. There are three types of releases:

NATURAL PRESSURE RELEASE

Let the pressure slowly release on its own, which can take anywhere from 5 to 25 minutes (but is typically in the 10- to 15-minute range). The release time will be shorter for an Express Crock that is less full and longer for one that is more full. When the bobber valve lowers, the pressure is released and you can open the lid.

QUICK PRESSURE RELEASE

Use a towel or pot holder to manually turn the steam release valve to the venting or open position immediately after the cooking is complete. Be sure to get out of the way of the steam, and position the pressure cooker on your countertop so the steam doesn't get expelled straight into your cabinets (or in your face). It can take up to 2 minutes to fully release all the pressure.

NATURAL/QUICK PRESSURE COMBINATION RELEASE

The recipe will instruct you to let the pressure release naturally for a certain amount of time (frequently for 10 to 15 minutes) and then do a quick release as directed.

RULES OF RELEASE

Releasing pressure can be a little confusing when you first start using an Express Crock. There's no need to worry at all about safety—you won't be able to open the lid until all the pressure has been released. And you don't need to guess which release to use since the recipes will tell you. But there are some important things to know about releasing pressure, especially when you start cooking and experimenting on your own.

Natural Pressure Release is best for meats (especially larger roasts and tough cuts), foods that generate a lot of foam, such as grains, dried beans and legumes, and foods that are primarily liquid, such as soups.

DONENESS TEMPERATURES

The best way to determine if meat is cooked properly is to test its internal temperature with an instant-read thermometer. To use an instant-read thermometer, insert it into the thickest part of the meat taking care not to poke it all the way through the meat and to avoid any bones. Leave the thermometer in the meat for about 20 seconds or until the needle stops moving. Instant-read thermometers are not heat-proof, so do not leave them in while cooking.

BEEF, LAMB OR VEAL

Ground Meat	165°F
Whole cuts	
Medium Rare	145°F
Medium	160°F
Well Done	170°F

CHICKEN, TURKEY OR OTHER POULTRY

Ground Chicken, Turkey or Other Poultry	165°F
Boneless Chicken Breasts	165°F
Whole or Bone-in Chicken or Poultry; Breast Meat	170°F
Whole or Bone-in Chicken or Poultry; Dark Meat	180°F

PORK

Ground Pork	165°F
Ham, Purchased Fully Cooked	140°F
Ham, Purchased Uncooked	170°F
Whole cuts	
Medium	155°F
Well-Done	170°F

THE CONTROL PANEL

The cooking functions you'll find on the control panel are convenient shortcuts for some foods you may prepare regularly (rice, beans, stews, etc.) which use preset times and cooking levels. In this book we'll explore the basics of pressure cooking with recipes that use customized cooking times and pressure levels. So you'll be able to cook a wide variety of delicious dishes.

If you're accustomed to a stovetop pressure cooker, you'll need to make a few minor adjustments when using an electric one. Electric pressure cookers regulate heat automatically, so there's no worry about adjusting the heat on a burner to maintain pressure. Also, electric pressure cookers operate at less than the conventional pressure standard of 15 pounds per square inch (psi) used by stovetop pressure cookers. Most electric pressure cookers operate at 9 to 11 psi, which means that stovetop pressure cooker recipes can be adapted to electric models by adding a little more cooking time.

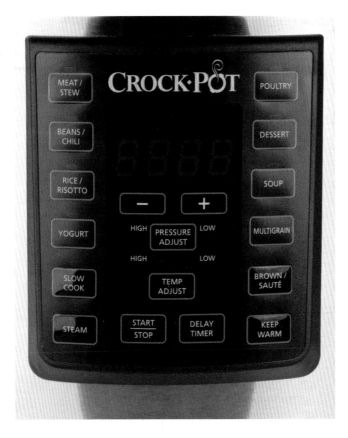

START/STOP

This button is used to start or stop a cooking program (such as when you are finished sautéing and are ready to start pressure cooking) or to turn off the Express Crock. When the chosen time for pressure cooking is complete, the Express Crock will automatically switch to the Keep Warm program.

BROWN/SAUTÉ

This function can be used to brown meats or to sauté vegetables. Browning meats before pressure cooking or slow cooking helps seal in juices and can help keep the meat tender. Sautéing vegetables contributes to the flavor and color of the end dish.

KEEP WARM

This function is used to keep cooked food warm until you're ready to serve, or to reheat food that has been allowed to cool. When the chosen time for pressure cooking is complete, the Express Crock will automatically switch to the KEEP WARM program.

SLOW COOK

The SLOW COOK function does not use pressure in the cooking process, but some pressure can build inside the unit during cooking. When using this function, ensure the Steam Release Valve is in the "Release" position. This function will cook similarly to standard slow cookers, using lower temperatures and longer cooking times.

STEAM

This function is perfect for gently steaming fish and vegetables. When steaming, use the steaming rack. The maximum capacity of liquid should be just under the rack wires, so that the liquid is not touching the food.

COOKING FUNCTION	DEFAULT SETTING	PRESSURE ADJUSTMENTS	TEMPERATURE ADJUSTMENTS	COOK TIME RANGE
MEAT/STEW	HIGH pressure/ 35 minutes	LOW-HIGH	N/A	15 minutes– 2 hours
BEANS/CHILI	HIGH pressure/ 20 minutes	LOW-HIGH	N/A	5 minutes– 2 hours
RICE/RISOTTO	LOW pressure/ 12 minutes	LOW-HIGH	N/A	6 minutes– 30 minutes
YOGURT	LOW temp/ 8 hours	N/A	LOW-HIGH	LOW: 6 hours– 12 hours
SLOW COOK	HIGH temp/ 4 hours	N/A	LOW-HIGH	30 minutes– 20 hours
STEAM	HIGH pressure/ 10 minutes	LOW-HIGH	N/A	3 minutes– 1 hour
POULTRY	HIGH pressure/ 15 minutes	LOW-HIGH	N/A	15 minutes– 2 hours
DESSERT	LOW pressure/ 10 minutes	LOW-HIGH	N/A	5 minutes– 2 hours
SOUP	HIGH pressure/ 30 minutes	LOW-HIGH	N/A	5 minutes– 2 hours
MULTIGRAIN	HIGH pressure/ 40 minutes	LOW-HIGH	N/A	10 minutes– 2 hours
BROWN/SAUTÉ	HIGH temp/ 30 minutes	N/A	LOW-HIGH	5 minutes– 30 minutes
KEEP WARM	Warm temp/ 4 hours	N/A	WARM	30 minutes– 4 hours

Quinoa Pilaf with
Shallot Vinaigrette
(*page 206*)

TIPS, TRICKS, DOS AND DON'TS

- Read the manual before beginning. There may be features you won't use, but it can help you understand how the machine works—and see all its possibilities.

- Don't overfill the Express Crock— the total amount of food and liquid should not exceed the maximum level marked on the inner cooking pot. Generally it is best not to fill the cooking pot more than two thirds full. When cooking foods that expand during cooking such as beans and grains, do not fill it more than half full.

- You do not need too many additional products when using the Express Crock, but a few simple kitchen items are useful for certain recipes. Heatproof containers such as soufflé dishes, baking dishes, ramekins or custard cups are often used to cook desserts that contain a lot of liquid, such as bread puddings or custards. They may be made of ceramic, metal, silicone or heatproof glass and should always be used with the steaming rack. In addition, foil handles (see diagram page 13) are recommended when using these containers to make lifting them from the Express Crock easier.

- Make sure there is always some liquid in the Express Crock before cooking because a minimum amount (usually 1 cup) is required to come up to pressure. (However, if the recipe contains a large amount of vegetables, you may be able to use a bit less since the vegetables will create their own liquid.)

- Always check that the pressure release valve is in the right position before you start pressure cooking. The food simply won't get cooked if the valve is not in the sealing or locked position because there will not be enough pressure in the Express Crock.

- Never try to force the lid open after cooking—if the lid won't open, that means the pressure has not fully released. (As a safety feature, the lid remains locked until the float valve drops down.)

- Save the thickeners for after the pressure or slow cooking is done. These recipes often end up with a lot of flavorful liquid left in the Express Crock when cooking is complete. Flour or cornstarch mixtures can thicken these liquids into delicious sauces. Use the BROWN/SAUTÉ function while incorporating the thickeners into the cooking liquid, and then cook and stir until the desired consistency is reached.

- Keep in mind that cooking times in some recipes may vary. These are approximate times and numerous variables may cause your results to be different. For example, the freshness of dried beans affects their cooking time (older beans take longer to cook), as does what they are cooked with—hard water (water that is high in mineral content), acidic ingredients, sugar and salt levels

Mediterranean Chili
(*page 82*)

can also affect cooking times. So be flexible and experiment with what works best for you—you can always check the doneness of your food and add more time.

- Set reasonable expectations, i.e., don't expect everything you cook in the Express Crock to be ready in a few minutes. Even though pressure cooking reduces many conventional cooking times dramatically, nothing is literally "fast"—it will always take time to get up to pressure, and then to release it. You can make fabulous pot roast, irresistible pulled pork, hearty soups, stews, chilies and risottos in a fraction of the time they might take on the stovetop. But if you're looking for casseroles with crispy toppings, charred meats and vegetables, or side dishes with crunch, then this is not the right machine for the job. Use the Express Crock for the types of recipes that work best, and then enjoy the time saved—and all the delicious results! The possibilities are endless!

FOIL HANDLES

To easily lift a dish or a meat loaf from a **CROCK-POT®** Express Crock Multi-Cooker, make foil handles as shown below.

1. Tear off three 18X2-inch strips of heavy-duty foil. Crisscross the strips so they resemble the spokes of a wheel. Place the dish of food in the center of the strips.

2. Pull the strips up and over the dish or food; using the foil handles, lift the dish or food and place it into the Express Crock. Leave the strips in during cooking so you can easily lift the item out again when it's ready.

Vegetable and
Red Lentil Soup (page 42)

SIMMERING SOUPS

CHICKEN STOCK

MAKES ABOUT 10 CUPS

1 cut-up whole chicken (4 to 6 pounds)

1 package (16 ounces) celery, cut into large pieces

1 large carrot, cut into 2- to 3-inch pieces

2 onions or leeks, quartered

2 large parsnips, coarsely chopped

½ cup loosely packed fresh herbs such as Italian parsley, dill, thyme, chervil or combination

Kosher salt and black pepper

1. Combine chicken, celery, carrot, onions, parsnips, herbs, salt and pepper in **CROCK-POT®** Express Crock Multi-Cooker. Add enough water to fill three-quarters full. Secure lid. Press SOUP, set pressure to HIGH and adjust time to 1 hour. Make sure the Steam Release Valve is in the "Seal" (closed) position. Press START/STOP.

2. Once cooking is complete, natural release pressure 15 minutes. Release remaining pressure; cool completely. Skim off and discard fat. Strain stock. (Shred chicken for another use or discard.) Place stock in storage containers; freeze up to 3 months.

1 cut-up whole chicken (4 to 6 pounds)

1 package (16 ounces) celery, cut into large pieces

1 large carrot, cut into 2- to 3-inch pieces

2 onions or leeks, quartered

2 large parsnips, coarsely chopped

½ cup loosely packed fresh herbs such as Italian parsley, dill, thyme, chervil or combination

Kosher salt and black pepper

1. Combine chicken, celery, carrot, onions, parsnips, herbs, salt and pepper in **CROCK-POT®** Express Crock Multi-Cooker. Add enough water to fill three-quarters full. Secure lid. Press SLOW COOK, set temperature and time to LOW 12 hours or to HIGH 8 hours. Make sure Steam Release Valve is in the "Release" (open) position. Press START/STOP.

2. Once cooking is complete, cool completely. Skim off and discard fat. Strain stock. (Shred chicken for another use or discard.) Place stock in storage containers; freeze up to 3 months.

BEEF STOCK

MAKES ABOUT 10 CUPS

FAST

2 tablespoons vegetable oil

3 to 4 pounds beef bones, preferably marrow or knuckle bones

2 large leeks, thoroughly cleaned and cut into 1-inch pieces

3 carrots, cut into 1-inch pieces

3 cups onions, coarsely chopped

2 stalks celery, cut into 1-inch pieces

2 sprigs fresh thyme

2 sprigs fresh Italian parsley

1 whole bay leaf

1½ teaspoons black peppercorns

1. Press BROWN/SAUTÉ on **CROCK-POT®** Express Crock Multi-Cooker; heat oil on HIGH. Add bones in batches; cook, uncovered, 3 to 4 minutes or until browned.

2. Add leeks, carrots, onions, celery, thyme, parsley, bay leaf and peppercorns to Express Crock. Add enough water to fill three-quarters full. Secure lid. Press SOUP, set pressure to HIGH and time to 1 hour. Make sure Steam Release Valve is in the "Seal" (closed) position. Press START/STOP.

3. Once cooking is complete, natural release pressure 15 minutes. Release remaining pressure; cool completely. Skim off and discard fat. Strain stock. Place stock in storage containers; freeze up to 3 months.

SLOW

2 tablespoons vegetable oil

3 to 4 pounds beef bones, preferably marrow or knuckle bones

2 large leeks, thoroughly cleaned and cut into 1-inch pieces

3 carrots, cut into 1-inch pieces

3 cups onions, coarsely chopped

2 stalks celery, cut into 1-inch pieces

2 sprigs fresh thyme

2 sprigs fresh Italian parsley

1 whole bay leaf

1½ teaspoons black peppercorns

1. Press BROWN/SAUTÉ on **CROCK-POT®** Express Crock Multi-Cooker; heat oil on HIGH. Add bones in batches; cook, uncovered, 3 to 4 minutes or until browned.

2. Add leeks, carrots, onions, celery, thyme, parsley, bay leaf and peppercorns to Express Crock. Add enough water to fill three-quarters full. Secure lid. Press SLOW COOK, set temperature and time to LOW 8 to 10 hours or to HIGH 5 to 6 hours. Make sure Steam Release Valve is in the "Release" (open) position. Press START/STOP.

3. Once cooking is complete, cool completely. Skim off and discard fat. Strain stock. Place stock in storage containers; freeze up to 3 months.

FISH STOCK

MAKES ABOUT 10 CUPS

FAST

2 tablespoons olive oil	1 cup dry white wine	4 sprigs fresh Italian parsley
1 large onion, chopped	2 whole tilapia fillets, scaled and gutted	4 whole black peppercorns
2 carrots, chopped	1 sprig fresh thyme	2 teaspoons salt
2 stalks celery, chopped		

1. Press BROWN/SAUTÉ on **CROCK-POT®** Express Crock Multi-Cooker; heat oil on HIGH. Add onion, carrots and celery; cook, uncovered, 3 minutes or until tender. Add wine, stirring to scrape up browned bits from bottom of Express Crock. Add tilapia, thyme, parsley, peppercorns and salt. Add enough water to fill three-quarters full. Secure lid. Press SOUP, set pressure to HIGH and time to 1 hour. Make sure the Steam Release Valve is in the "Seal" (closed) position. Press START/STOP.

2. Once cooking is complete, natural release pressure 15 minutes. Release remaining pressure; cool completely. Skim off and discard fat. Strain stock. Place stock in storage containers; freeze up to 3 months.

SLOW

2 tablespoons olive oil	1 cup dry white wine	4 sprigs fresh Italian parsley
1 large onion, chopped	2 whole tilapia fillets, scaled and gutted	4 whole black peppercorns
2 carrots, chopped	1 sprig fresh thyme	2 teaspoons salt
2 stalks celery, chopped		

1. Press BROWN/SAUTÉ on **CROCK-POT®** Express Crock Multi-Cooker; heat oil on HIGH. Add onion, carrots and celery; cook, uncovered, 3 minutes or until tender. Add wine, stirring to scrape up browned bits from bottom of Express Crock. Add tilapia, thyme, parsley, peppercorns and salt. Add enough water to fill three-quarters full. Secure lid. Press SLOW COOK, set temperature to HIGH and time to 3½ hours. Make sure Steam Release Valve is in the "Release" (open) position. Press START/STOP.

2. Once cooking is complete, cool completely. Skim off and discard fat. Strain stock. Place stock in storage containers; freeze up to 3 months.

VEGETABLE STOCK

MAKES ABOUT 10 CUPS

FAST

3 carrots, coarsely chopped

3 parsnips, coarsely chopped

3 onions, quartered

3 leeks, coarsely chopped

3 stalks celery, coarsely chopped

3 whole bay leaves

2 sprigs fresh thyme

4 sprigs fresh Italian parsley

8 whole black peppercorns

Kosher salt

Water

1. Add carrots, parsnips, onions, leeks, celery, bay leaves, thyme, parsley, peppercorns and salt to **CROCK-POT®** Express Crock Multi-Cooker. Add enough water to fill three-quarters full. Secure lid. Press SOUP, set temperature to HIGH and time to 1 hour. Make sure Steam Release Valve is in the "Seal" (closed) position. Press START/STOP.

2. Once cooking is complete, natural release pressure 15 minutes. Release remaining pressure; cool completely. Skim off and discard fat. Strain stock. Place stock in storage containers; freeze up to 3 months.

SLOW

3 carrots, coarsely chopped

3 parsnips, coarsely chopped

3 onions, quartered

3 leeks, coarsely chopped

3 stalks celery, coarsely chopped

3 whole bay leaves

2 sprigs fresh thyme

4 sprigs fresh Italian parsley

8 whole black peppercorns

Kosher salt

Water

1. Add carrots, parsnips, onions, leeks, celery, bay leaves, thyme, parsley, peppercorns and salt to **CROCK-POT®** Express Crock Multi-Cooker. Add enough water to fill three-quarters full. Secure lid. Press SLOW COOK, set temperature and time to LOW 10 to 12 hours or to HIGH 6 to 8 hours. Make sure Steam Release Valve is in the "Release" (open) position. Press START/STOP.

2. Once cooking is complete, cool completely. Skim off and discard fat. Strain stock. Place stock in storage containers; freeze up to 3 months.

HEARTY CHICKEN TEQUILA SOUP

MAKES 4 SERVINGS

FAST

1½ pounds boneless, skinless chicken thighs

3 cups chicken broth

1 can (about 14 ounces) diced tomatoes with mild green chiles

1 cup frozen corn

1 small onion, cut into 8 wedges

¼ cup tequila

2 cloves garlic, minced

¼ cup sour cream

Chopped fresh cilantro (optional)

1. Combine chicken, broth, tomatoes, corn, onion, tequila and garlic in **CROCK-POT®** Express Crock Multi-Cooker. Secure lid. Press SOUP, set pressure to HIGH and time to 15 minutes. Make sure Steam Release Valve is in the "Seal" (closed) position. Press START/STOP.

2. Once cooking is complete, natural release pressure 10 minutes. Release remaining pressure. Remove chicken to large cutting board; shred with two forks. Stir shredded chicken back into Express Crock. Ladle into individual bowls. Top each serving with sour cream; garnish with cilantro.

SLOW

1 small onion, cut into 8 wedges

1 cup frozen corn

1 can (about 14 ounces) diced tomatoes with mild green chiles

2 cloves garlic, minced

2 tablespoons chopped fresh cilantro, plus additional for garnish

1½ pounds boneless, skinless chicken thighs

2 cups chicken broth

3 tablespoons tequila

¼ cup sour cream

1. Place onion wedges on bottom of **CROCK-POT®** Express Crock Multi-Cooker. Add corn, tomatoes, garlic and 2 tablespoons cilantro; stir to blend. Place chicken on top of tomato mixture. Pour broth and tequila over chicken and tomato mixture. Secure lid. Press SLOW COOK, set temperature to LOW and time to 8 hours. Make sure Steam Release Valve is in the "Release" (open) position. Press START/STOP.

2. Once cooking is complete, remove chicken to large cutting board; shred chicken with two forks. Stir shredded chicken back into Express Crock. Ladle into individual bowls. Top each serving with sour cream; garnish with additional cilantro.

SMOKED SAUSAGE AND BEAN SOUP

MAKES 9 SERVINGS

FAST

- 1 link (about 6 ounces) mild Italian sausage, casing removed
- 4 cups chicken broth
- 1 cup dried black beans, rinsed and sorted
- 1 cup chopped yellow onion

- 2 whole bay leaves
- 1 teaspoon sugar
- 1/8 teaspoon ground red pepper
- 1 cup chopped tomato
- 1 tablespoon Worcestershire sauce

- 2 teaspoons extra virgin olive oil
- 1 tablespoon chili powder
- 1 1/2 teaspoons ground cumin
- 1/2 teaspoon salt
- 1/4 cup chopped fresh cilantro

1. Press BROWN/SAUTÉ on **CROCK-POT®** Express Crock Multi-Cooker. Add sausage; cook on HIGH 8 minutes, stirring to break up meat. Drain fat.

2. Combine sausage, broth, beans, onion, bay leaves, sugar and ground red pepper in Express Crock. Secure lid. Press BEANS/CHILI, set pressure to HIGH and time to 23 minutes. Make sure Steam Release Valve is in the "Release" (open) position. Press START/STOP.

3. Once cooking is complete, natural release pressure 10 minutes. Release remaining pressure. Press BROWN/SAUTÉ on Express Crock. Stir in tomato, Worcestershire sauce, oil, chili powder, cumin and salt; cook, uncovered, on HIGH 15 minutes. Sprinkle each serving with cilantro.

SLOW

- 1 link (about 6 ounces) mild Italian sausage, casing removed
- 2 cans (about 14 ounces each) chicken broth
- 1 1/2 cups hot water
- 1 cup dried black beans, rinsed and sorted

- 1 cup chopped yellow onion
- 2 whole bay leaves
- 1 teaspoon sugar
- 1/8 teaspoon ground red pepper
- 1 cup chopped tomato
- 1 tablespoon Worcestershire sauce

- 2 teaspoons extra virgin olive oil
- 1 tablespoon chili powder
- 1 1/2 teaspoons ground cumin
- 1/2 teaspoon salt
- 1/4 cup chopped fresh cilantro

1. Press BROWN/SAUTÉ on **CROCK-POT®** Express Crock Multi-Cooker. Add sausage; cook on HIGH 8 minutes, stirring to break up meat. Drain fat.

2. Combine sausage, broth, water, beans, onion, bay leaves, sugar and ground red pepper in Express Crock. Secure lid. Press SLOW COOK, set temperature and time to LOW 8 hours or to HIGH 4 hours. Make sure Steam Release Valve is in the "Release" (open) position. Press START/STOP.

3. Once cooking is complete, press BROWN/SAUTÉ on Express Crock. Stir in tomato, Worcestershire sauce, oil, chili powder, cumin and salt; cook, uncovered, on HIGH 15 minutes. Sprinkle each serving with cilantro.

MEDITERRANEAN BEAN SOUP WITH ORZO AND FETA

MAKES 6 SERVINGS

FAST

1 can (about 15 ounces) chickpeas, rinsed and drained

1 can (about 14 ounces) Italian-style diced tomatoes

1 can (about 14 ounces) vegetable broth

1 package (10 ounces) frozen mixed carrots and peas

½ cup uncooked orzo pasta

2 teaspoons dried oregano

½ cup crumbled feta cheese

Salt and black pepper

1. Combine chickpeas, tomatoes, broth, carrots and peas, pasta and oregano in **CROCK-POT®** Express Crock Multi-Cooker. Secure lid. Press SOUP, set pressure to HIGH and time to 10 minutes. Make sure Steam Release Valve is in the "Seal" (closed) position. Press START/STOP.

2. Once cooking is complete, natural release pressure 10 minutes. Release remaining pressure. Top each serving with cheese; season with salt and pepper.

SLOW

1 can (about 15 ounces) chickpeas, rinsed and drained

1 can (about 14 ounces) Italian-style diced tomatoes

1 can (about 14 ounces) vegetable broth

1 package (10 ounces) frozen mixed carrots and peas

½ cup uncooked orzo pasta

2 teaspoons dried oregano

½ cup crumbled feta cheese

Salt and black pepper

1. Combine chickpeas, tomatoes, broth, carrots and peas, pasta and oregano in **CROCK-POT®** Express Crock Multi-Cooker. Secure lid. Press SLOW COOK, set temperature and time to LOW 5 to 6 hours or to HIGH 2 to 3 hours. Make sure Steam Release Valve is in the "Release" (open) position. Press START/STOP.

2. Once cooking is complete, top each serving with cheese. Season with salt and pepper.

COUNTRY TURKEY AND VEGGIE SOUP WITH CREAM

MAKES 8 SERVINGS

FAST

2 tablespoons butter, divided

8 ounces sliced mushrooms

1/2 cup chopped onion

4 cups turkey or chicken broth

1 red bell pepper, chopped

1 stalk celery, thinly sliced

1 carrot, thinly sliced

1/2 teaspoon dried thyme

2 cups chopped cooked turkey

4 ounces uncooked egg noodles

1 cup half-and-half

1/2 cup frozen peas, thawed

3/4 teaspoon salt

1. Press BROWN/SAUTÉ on **CROCK-POT®** Express Crock Multi-Cooker; melt 1 tablespoon butter on HIGH. Add mushrooms and onion; cook and stir 4 minutes or until onion is softened. Add broth, bell pepper, celery, carrot and thyme. Secure lid. Press POULTRY, set pressure to HIGH and time to 15 minutes. Make sure Steam Release Valve is in the "Seal" (closed) position. Press START/STOP.

2. Once cooking is complete, quick release pressure. Stir in turkey. Press BROWN/SAUTÉ on Express Crock; bring soup to a boil on HIGH. Add noodles; cook, uncovered, 8 minutes or until tender. Stir in half-and-half, peas, remaining 1 tablespoon butter and salt; cook, uncovered, 2 minutes or until heated through.

SLOW

2 tablespoons butter, divided

8 ounces sliced mushrooms

1/2 cup chopped onion

4 cups turkey or chicken broth

1 red bell pepper, chopped

1 stalk celery, thinly sliced

1 carrot, thinly sliced

1/2 teaspoon dried thyme

2 cups chopped cooked turkey

4 ounces uncooked egg noodles

1 cup half-and-half

1/2 cup frozen peas, thawed

3/4 teaspoon salt

1. Press BROWN/SAUTÉ on **CROCK-POT®** Express Crock Multi-Cooker; melt 1 tablespoon butter on HIGH. Add mushrooms and onion; cook and stir 4 minutes or until onion is softened. Add broth, bell pepper, celery, carrot and thyme. Secure lid. Press SLOW COOK, set temperature to HIGH and time to 2 1/2 hours. Make sure Steam Release Valve is in the "Release" (open) position. Press START/STOP.

2. Once cooking is complete, stir in turkey. Press BROWN/SAUTÉ on Express Crock; bring soup to a boil on HIGH. Add noodles; cook, uncovered, 8 minutes or until tender. Stir in half-and-half, peas, remaining 1 tablespoon butter and salt; cook, uncovered, 2 minutes or until heated through.

TOMATO SOUP WITH DITALINI

MAKES 6 SERVINGS

FAST

2 cans (28 ounces *each*) whole plum tomatoes

4 cups vegetable broth

1 medium onion, chopped (about 1 cup)

½ medium bulb fennel, chopped (about 1 cup)

2 carrots, chopped (about 1 cup)

3 tablespoons tomato paste

3 cloves garlic, minced

1 teaspoon dried basil

1 teaspoon salt

¼ teaspoon black pepper

3 cups hot cooked ditalini pasta

Grated Parmesan cheese

1. Combine tomatoes, broth, onion, fennel, carrots, tomato paste, garlic, basil, salt and pepper in **CROCK-POT®** Express Crock Multi-Cooker; stir to blend. Secure lid. Press SOUP, set pressure to HIGH and time to 10 minutes. Make sure Steam Release Valve is in the "Seal" (closed) position. Press START/STOP.

2. Once cooking is complete, natural release pressure 10 minutes. Release remaining pressure. Remove soup in batches to food processor or blender; process until smooth. To serve, place ½ cup pasta into each of six bowls; top with soup. Sprinkle with cheese.

SLOW

2 cans (28 ounces *each*) whole plum tomatoes

4 cups vegetable broth

1 medium onion, chopped (about 1 cup)

½ medium bulb fennel, chopped (about 1 cup)

2 carrots, chopped (about 1 cup)

3 tablespoons tomato paste

3 cloves garlic, minced

1 teaspoon dried basil

1 teaspoon salt

¼ teaspoon black pepper

3 cups hot cooked ditalini pasta

Grated Parmesan cheese

1. Combine tomatoes, broth, onion, fennel, carrots, tomato paste, garlic, basil, salt and pepper in **CROCK-POT®** Express Crock Multi-Cooker; stir to blend. Secure lid. Press SLOW COOK, set temperature and time to LOW 7 to 8 hours or to HIGH 3 to 4 hours. Make sure Steam Release Valve is in the "Release" (open) position. Press START/STOP.

2. Once cooking is complete, remove soup in batches to food processor or blender; process until smooth. To serve, place ½ cup pasta into each of six bowls; top with soup. Sprinkle with cheese.

NEW ENGLAND CLAM CHOWDER

MAKES 6 TO 8 SERVINGS

FAST

3 slices bacon, diced

2 medium onions, chopped

5 cans (6½ ounces *each*) clams, drained and liquid reserved

6 medium red potatoes, cubed

2 tablespoons minced garlic

1 teaspoon black pepper

2 cans (12 ounces *each*) evaporated milk

Snipped fresh chives (optional)

1. Press BROWN/SAUTÉ on **CROCK-POT®** Express Crock Multi-Cooker. Add bacon and onions; cook and stir on HIGH 5 to 7 minutes or until bacon is crisp and onion is softened.

2. Add enough water to reserved clam liquid to make 3 cups; pour into Express Crock. Add potatoes, garlic and pepper. Secure lid. Press SOUP, set pressure to HIGH and time to 5 minutes. Make sure Steam Release Valve is in the "Seal" (closed) position. Press START/STOP.

3. Once cooking is complete, quick release pressure. Press BROWN/SAUTÉ on Express Crock. Add clams and evaporated milk; cook and stir 3 minutes or until heated through. Garnish each serving with chives.

SLOW

3 slices bacon, diced

2 medium onions, chopped

5 cans (6½ ounces *each*) clams, drained and liquid reserved

6 medium red potatoes, cubed

2 tablespoons minced garlic

1 teaspoon black pepper

2 cans (12 ounces *each*) evaporated milk

Snipped fresh chives (optional)

1. Press BROWN/SAUTÉ on **CROCK-POT®** Express Crock Multi-Cooker. Add bacon and onions; cook and stir on HIGH 5 to 7 minutes or until bacon is crisp and onion is softened.

2. Add enough water to reserved clam liquid to make 3 cups; pour into Express Crock. Add potatoes, garlic and pepper. Secure lid. Press SLOW COOK, set temperature and time to LOW 4 to 8 hours or to HIGH 2 to 4 hours. Make sure Steam Release Valve is in the "Release" (open) position. Press START/STOP.

3. Once cooking is complete, press BROWN/SAUTÉ on Express Crock. Add clams and evaporated milk; cook and stir 3 minutes or until heated through. Garnish each serving with chives.

BEEF, LENTIL AND ONION SOUP

MAKES 4 SERVINGS

1 tablespoon olive oil	1 cup sliced celery	3¼ cups water
¾ pound cubed beef stew meat	1 cup uncooked lentils	1 can (about 10 ounces) condensed French onion soup, undiluted
2 cups chopped carrots	2 teaspoons dried thyme	
1 medium onion, chopped	¼ teaspoon black pepper	
	⅛ teaspoon salt	

1. Press BROWN/SAUTÉ on **CROCK-POT®** Express Crock Multi-Cooker; heat oil on HIGH. Add beef; cook 5 to 7 minutes or until browned. Add carrots, onion, celery and lentils to Express Crock. Sprinkle with thyme, pepper and salt. Pour water and soup into Express Crock.

2. Secure lid. Press BEANS/CHILI, set pressure to HIGH and time to 20 minutes. Make sure Steam Release Valve is in the "Seal" (closed) position. Press START/STOP.

3. Once cooking is complete, natural release pressure 10 minutes. Release remaining pressure. Serve in individual bowls.

1 tablespoon olive oil	1 cup sliced celery	3¼ cups water
¾ pound cubed beef stew meat	1 cup uncooked lentils	1 can (about 10 ounces) condensed French onion soup, undiluted
2 cups chopped carrots	2 teaspoons dried thyme	
1 medium onion, chopped	¼ teaspoon black pepper	
	⅛ teaspoon salt	

1. Press BROWN/SAUTÉ on **CROCK-POT®** Express Crock Multi-Cooker; heat oil on HIGH. Add beef; cook 5 to 7 minutes or until browned. Add carrots, onion, celery and lentils to Express Crock. Sprinkle with thyme, pepper and salt. Pour water and soup into Express Crock.

2. Secure lid. Press SLOW COOK, set temperature and time to LOW 7 to 8 hours or to HIGH 3½ to 4 hours. Make sure Steam Release Valve is in the "Release" (open) position. Press START/STOP.

3. Once cooking is complete, serve in individual bowls.

SPICY THAI COCONUT SOUP

MAKES 4 SERVINGS

FAST

2 boneless, skinless chicken breasts (about 1 pound)

1 cup chicken broth

1 can (15 ounces) straw mushrooms, drained

1 can (13½ ounces) unsweetened coconut milk

1 can (about 8 ounces) baby corn, drained

2 tablespoons lime juice

1 tablespoon minced fresh ginger

½ to 1 teaspoon red curry paste*

¼ cup chopped fresh cilantro

Red curry paste can be found in jars in the Asian food section of large grocery stores. Spice levels can vary between brands. Start with ½ teaspoon, then add more as desired.

1. Combine chicken and broth in **CROCK-POT®** Express Crock Multi-Cooker. Secure lid. Press POULTRY, set pressure to HIGH and time to 20 minutes. Make sure Steam Release Valve is in the "Seal" (closed) position. Press START/STOP.

2. Once cooking is complete, natural release pressure 10 minutes. Release remaining pressure. Remove chicken to large cutting board; shred with two forks. Press BROWN/SAUTÉ on Express Crock. Add shredded chicken, mushrooms, coconut milk, corn, lime juice, ginger and curry paste to Express Crock; cook and stir, uncovered, on HIGH 3 to 5 minutes or until heated through. Sprinkle each serving with cilantro just before serving.

SLOW

3 cups coarsely shredded cooked chicken (about 12 ounces)

2 cups chicken broth

1 can (15 ounces) straw mushrooms, drained

1 can (13½ ounces) unsweetened coconut milk

1 can (about 8 ounces) baby corn, drained

1 tablespoon minced fresh ginger

½ to 1 teaspoon red curry paste*

2 tablespoons lime juice

¼ cup chopped fresh cilantro

Red curry paste can be found in jars in the Asian food section of large grocery stores. Spice levels can vary between brands. Start with ½ teaspoon, then add more as desired.

1. Combine chicken, broth, mushrooms, coconut milk, corn, ginger and curry paste in **CROCK-POT®** Express Crock Multi-Cooker. Secure lid. Press SLOW COOK, set temperature to HIGH and time to 2 to 3 hours. Make sure Steam Release Valve is in the "Release" (open) position. Press START/STOP.

2. Once cooking is complete, stir in lime juice and sprinkle each serving with cilantro just before serving.

MEDITERRANEAN TOMATO, OREGANO AND ORZO SOUP

MAKES 6 SERVINGS

FAST

2 tablespoons extra virgin olive oil

1 large yellow onion, cut into wedges

3½ cups fresh tomatoes, peeled and crushed*

2 cups butternut squash, cut into 1-inch cubes

4 cups chicken broth, divided

1 can (about 15 ounces) chickpeas, rinsed and drained

1 cup carrots, cut into matchstick pieces

½ cup zucchini, sliced

3 whole bay leaves

1 tablespoon chopped fresh oregano

1 clove garlic, minced

1 teaspoon ground cumin

¾ teaspoon ground allspice

½ teaspoon salt

¼ teaspoon black pepper

¾ cup uncooked orzo pasta

To peel tomatoes, place one at a time in simmering water about 10 seconds. (Add 30 seconds if tomatoes are not fully ripened.) Immediately plunge into a bowl of cold water for another 10 seconds. Peel skin with a knife.

1. Press BROWN/SAUTÉ on **CROCK-POT®** Express Crock Multi-Cooker; heat oil on HIGH. Add onion; cook and stir about 10 minutes or until translucent. Add tomatoes, squash, 2 cups broth, chickpeas, carrots, zucchini, bay leaves, oregano, garlic, cumin, allspice, salt and pepper to Express Crock. Secure lid. Press SOUP, set pressure to HIGH and time to 7 minutes. Make sure Steam Release Valve is in the "Seal" (closed) position. Press START/STOP.

2. Once cooking is complete, quick release pressure. Press BROWN/SAUTÉ on Express Crock. Add orzo and remaining 2 cups broth; cook and stir on LOW 10 minutes or until orzo is cooked through. Remove and discard bay leaves.

SLOW

2 tablespoons extra virgin olive oil

1 large yellow onion, cut into wedges

3½ cups fresh tomatoes, peeled and crushed*

2 cups butternut squash, cut into ½-inch cubes

4 cups chicken broth, divided

1 can (about 15 ounces) chickpeas, rinsed and drained

1 cup carrots, cut into matchstick pieces

½ cup zucchini, sliced

3 whole bay leaves

1 tablespoon chopped fresh oregano

1 clove garlic, minced

1 teaspoon ground cumin

¾ teaspoon ground allspice

½ teaspoon salt

¼ teaspoon black pepper

¾ cup uncooked orzo pasta

To peel tomatoes, place one at a time in simmering water about 10 seconds. (Add 30 seconds if tomatoes are not fully ripened.) Immediately plunge into a bowl of cold water for another 10 seconds. Peel skin with a knife.

1. Press BROWN/SAUTÉ on **CROCK-POT®** Express Crock Multi-Cooker; heat oil on HIGH. Add onion; cook and stir about 10 minutes or until translucent. Add tomatoes, squash, 2 cups broth, chickpeas, carrots, zucchini, bay leaves, oregano, garlic, cumin, allspice, salt and pepper to Express Crock. Secure lid. Press SLOW COOK, set temperature and time to LOW 7 to 8 hours or to HIGH 4 to 5 hours. Make sure Steam Release Valve is in the "Release" (open) position. Press START/STOP.

2. Once cooking is complete, press BROWN/SAUTÉ on Express Crock. Add orzo and remaining 2 cups broth; cook and stir on LOW 10 minutes or until orzo is cooked through. Remove and discard bay leaves.

THAI COCONUT CHICKEN AND RICE SOUP

MAKES 6 TO 8 SERVINGS

FAST

- 3 cups chicken broth
- 1 pound boneless, skinless chicken thighs, cut into 1-inch pieces
- 1 package (12 ounces) frozen chopped onions
- 1/2 medium red bell pepper, seeded and thinly sliced
- 1 can (4 ounces) sliced mushrooms, drained
- 2 tablespoons sugar
- 2 tablespoons minced fresh ginger
- 1/2 cup uncooked rice
- 1 can (13 1/2 ounces) unsweetened coconut milk
- 3 tablespoons chopped fresh cilantro
- 2 tablespoons grated lime peel

1. Combine broth, chicken, onions, bell pepper, mushrooms, sugar and ginger in **CROCK-POT®** Express Crock Multi-Cooker. Secure lid. Press POULTRY, set pressure to HIGH and time to 15 minutes. Make sure Steam Release Valve is in the "Seal" (closed) position. Press START/STOP.

2. Once cooking is complete, quick release pressure. Press BROWN/SAUTÉ on Express Crock. Add rice, coconut milk, cilantro and lime peel; cook and stir on HIGH 3 to 5 minutes or until heated through.

SLOW

- 3 cups chicken broth
- 1 pound boneless, skinless chicken thighs, cut into 1-inch pieces
- 1 package (12 ounces) frozen chopped onions
- 1/2 medium red bell pepper, seeded and thinly sliced
- 1 can (4 ounces) sliced mushrooms, drained
- 2 tablespoons sugar
- 2 tablespoons minced fresh ginger
- 1/2 cup cooked rice
- 1 can (13 1/2 ounces) unsweetened coconut milk
- 3 tablespoons chopped fresh cilantro
- 2 tablespoons grated lime peel

1. Combine broth, chicken, onions, bell pepper, mushrooms, sugar and ginger in **CROCK-POT®** Express Crock Multi-Cooker. Secure lid. Press SLOW COOK, set temperature to LOW and time to 8 to 9 hours. Make sure Steam Release Valve is in the "Release" (open) position. Press START/STOP.

2. Once cooking is complete, press BROWN/SAUTÉ on Express Crock. Add rice, coconut milk, cilantro and lime peel; cook and stir on HIGH 3 to 5 minutes or until heated through.

ITALIAN HILLSIDE GARDEN SOUP

MAKES 6 SERVINGS

FAST

1 tablespoon olive oil

1 cup chopped onion

1 cup chopped green bell pepper

½ cup sliced celery

2 cans (about 14 ounces *each*) chicken broth

1 can (about 15 ounces) cannellini beans, rinsed and drained

1 can (about 14 ounces) diced tomatoes with basil, garlic and oregano

1 package (9 ounces) refrigerated sausage- or cheese-filled tortellini

1 medium zucchini, chopped

1 cup frozen cut green beans, thawed

¼ teaspoon garlic powder

3 tablespoons chopped fresh basil

Grated Asiago or Parmesan cheese (optional)

1. Press BROWN/SAUTÉ on **CROCK-POT**® Express Crock Multi-Cooker; heat oil on HIGH. Add onion, bell pepper and celery; cook and stir 4 minutes or until onion is translucent. Add broth, cannellini beans, tomatoes, tortellini, zucchini, green beans and garlic powder. Secure lid. Press SOUP, set pressure to HIGH and time to 10 minutes. Make sure Steam Release Valve is in the "Seal" (closed) position. Press START/STOP.

2. Once cooking is complete, quick release pressure. Stir in basil. Sprinkle with cheese, if desired, just before serving.

SLOW

1 tablespoon olive oil

1 cup chopped onion

1 cup chopped green bell pepper

½ cup sliced celery

2 cans (about 14 ounces *each*) chicken broth

1 can (about 15 ounces) cannellini beans, rinsed and drained

1 can (about 14 ounces) diced tomatoes with basil, garlic and oregano

1 package (9 ounces) refrigerated sausage- or cheese-filled tortellini

1 medium zucchini, chopped

1 cup frozen cut green beans, thawed

¼ teaspoon garlic powder

3 tablespoons chopped fresh basil

Grated Asiago or Parmesan cheese (optional)

1. Press BROWN/SAUTÉ on **CROCK-POT**® Express Crock Multi-Cooker; heat oil on HIGH. Add onion, bell pepper and celery; cook and stir 4 minutes or until onion is translucent. Add broth, cannellini beans, tomatoes, tortellini, zucchini, green beans and garlic powder. Secure lid. Press SLOW COOK, set temperature and time to LOW 7 hours or to HIGH 3½ hours. Make sure Steam Release Valve is in the "Release" (open) position. Press START/STOP.

2. Once cooking is complete, stir in basil. Sprinkle with cheese, if desired, just before serving.

VEGETABLE AND RED LENTIL SOUP

MAKES 6 SERVINGS

FAST

2 tablespoons oil

1 red or yellow bell pepper, chopped

½ cup thinly sliced carrot

3 cups vegetable broth

½ cup dried red lentils, rinsed and sorted

½ teaspoon salt

½ teaspoon sugar

¼ teaspoon black pepper

2 medium zucchini or yellow summer squash, chopped

1 medium tomato, chopped

2 tablespoons chopped fresh basil (optional)

1. Press BROWN/SAUTÉ on **CROCK-POT®** Express Crock Multi-Cooker; heat oil on HIGH. Add bell pepper and carrot; cook and stir 3 minutes or until softened. Add broth, lentils, salt, sugar and black pepper to Express Crock; stir to blend. Secure lid. Press SOUP, set pressure to HIGH and time to 15 minutes. Make sure Steam Release Valve is in the "Seal" (closed) position. Press START/STOP.

2. Once cooking is complete, natural release pressure 10 minutes. Release remaining pressure. Press BROWN/SAUTÉ on Express Crock. Stir in zucchini and tomato; cook on LOW, uncovered, 5 minutes or until heated through. Sprinkle each serving with basil, if desired.

SLOW

1 can (about 14 ounces) vegetable broth

1 can (about 14 ounces) diced tomatoes

2 medium zucchini or yellow summer squash, chopped

1 red or yellow bell pepper, chopped

½ cup thinly sliced carrot

½ cup dried red lentils, rinsed and sorted

½ teaspoon salt

½ teaspoon sugar

¼ teaspoon black pepper

2 tablespoons chopped fresh basil (optional)

1. Combine broth, tomatoes, zucchini, bell pepper, carrot, lentils, salt, sugar and black pepper in **CROCK-POT®** Express Crock Multi-Cooker; stir to blend. Secure lid. Press SLOW COOK, set temperature and time to LOW 8 hours or to HIGH 4 hours. Make sure Steam Release Valve is in the "Release" (open) position. Press START/STOP.

2. Once cooking is complete, sprinkle each serving with basil, if desired.

LEEK AND POTATO SOUP

MAKES 4 TO 6 SERVINGS

FAST

6 slices chopped bacon

3 leeks, halved lengthwise and cut into ³/₄-inch pieces (white and light green parts only)

2 stalks celery, sliced

3 to 4 large baking potatoes, peeled and cut into ³/₄-inch pieces (about 5 cups)

1 can (about 14 ounces) chicken broth

1 can (10³/₄ ounces) condensed cream of potato soup, undiluted

1 can (5 ounces) evaporated milk

¹/₂ cup sour cream

1. Press BROWN/SAUTÉ on **CROCK-POT®** Express Crock Multi-Cooker. Add bacon; cook and stir 10 minutes or until crisp. Drain all but 1 tablespoon drippings. Reserve 2 tablespoons bacon. Layer leeks, celery and potatoes in Express Crock. Add broth; *do not stir.* Secure lid. Press SOUP, set pressure to HIGH and time to 6 minutes. Make sure Steam Release Valve is in the "Seal" (closed) position. Press START/STOP.

2. Once cooking is complete, quick release pressure. Slightly mash with potato masher. Stir in soup, evaporated milk and sour cream. Sprinkle each serving evenly with reserved bacon.

SLOW

6 slices chopped bacon

3 leeks, halved lengthwise and cut into ³/₄-inch pieces (white and light green parts only)

2 stalks celery, sliced

3 to 4 large baking potatoes, cut into ³/₄-inch pieces (about 5 cups)

1 can (about 14 ounces) chicken broth

1 can (10³/₄ ounces) condensed cream of potato soup, undiluted

1 can (5 ounces) evaporated milk

¹/₂ cup sour cream

1. Press BROWN/SAUTÉ on **CROCK-POT®** Express Crock Multi-Cooker. Add bacon; cook and stir 10 minutes until crisp. Drain all but 1 tablespoon drippings. Reserve 2 tablespoons bacon. Layer leeks, celery and potatoes in Express Crock. Add broth; *do not stir.* Secure lid. Press SLOW COOK, set temperature to LOW and time to 6 to 7 hours. Make sure Steam Release Valve is in the "Release" (open) position. Press START/STOP.

2. Once cooking is complete, slightly mash with potato masher. Stir in soup, evaporated milk and sour cream. Sprinkle each serving evenly with reserved bacon.

CURRIED LAMB AND SWISS CHARD SOUP

MAKES 6 TO 8 SERVINGS

- 2 tablespoons extra virgin olive oil
- 1 small red onion, chopped
- 2 cloves garlic, minced
- 8 cups chicken broth
- 2 cups cannellini beans, rinsed and sorted
- 2 lamb shanks
- 1½ teaspoons salt
- 1 teaspoon curry powder
- 1 teaspoon black pepper
- 2 cups Swiss chard, trimmed, cleaned and chopped
- 2 cups green cabbage, cored, cleaned and chopped
- ¼ cup lemon juice
- 1 teaspoon grated lemon peel (optional)
- Chopped fresh Italian parsley (optional)

1. Press BROWN/SAUTÉ on **CROCK-POT®** Express Crock Multi-Cooker; heat oil on HIGH. Add onion and garlic; cook and stir 3 to 4 minutes or until tender. Add broth, beans, lamb shanks, salt, curry powder and pepper to Express Crock; stir to blend. Secure lid. Press MEAT/STEW, set pressure to HIGH and time to 45 minutes. Make sure Steam Release Valve is in the "Seal" (closed) position. Press START/STOP.

2. Once cooking is complete, natural release pressure 10 minutes. Release remaining pressure. Remove lamb shanks to large cutting board; let stand 10 minutes. Remove and discard bones; shred meat using two forks.

3. Add Swiss chard and cabbage to Express Crock. Secure lid. Press STEAM, set pressure to HIGH and time to 5 minutes. Make sure Steam Release Valve is in the "Seal" (closed) position. Press START/STOP.

4. Once cooking is complete, quick release pressure. Add shredded meat and lemon juice to Express Crock; stir to blend. Garnish each serving with lemon peel and parsley.

- 2 tablespoons extra virgin olive oil
- 1 small red onion, chopped
- 2 cloves garlic, minced
- 8 cups chicken broth
- 2 cups Swiss chard, trimmed, cleaned and chopped
- 2 cups green cabbage, cored, cleaned and chopped
- 2 cups cannellini beans, rinsed and sorted
- 2 lamb shanks
- 1½ teaspoons salt
- 1 teaspoon curry powder
- 1 teaspoon black pepper
- ¼ cup lemon juice
- 1 teaspoon grated lemon peel (optional)
- Chopped fresh Italian parsley (optional)

1. Press BROWN/SAUTÉ on **CROCK-POT®** Express Crock Multi-Cooker; heat oil on HIGH. Add onion and garlic; cook and stir 3 to 4 minutes or until tender. Add broth, Swiss chard, cabbage, beans, lamb shanks, salt, curry powder and pepper to Express Crock; stir to blend. Secure lid. Press SLOW COOK, set temperature to LOW and time to 8 to 10 hours. Make sure Steam Release Valve is in the "Release" (open) position. Press START/STOP.

2. Once cooking is complete, remove lamb shanks to large cutting board. Let stand 10 minutes. Remove and discard bones from meat; shred meat. Add shredded meat and lemon juice to Express Crock; stir to blend. Garnish each serving with lemon peel and parsley.

NORTHWEST BEEF AND VEGETABLE SOUP

MAKES 6 TO 8 SERVINGS

FAST

- 2 tablespoons olive oil
- 1 pound cubed beef stew meat
- 1 medium onion, chopped
- 1 clove garlic, minced
- 6 cups water
- 3½ cups canned crushed tomatoes, undrained
- 1 butternut squash, cut into 1-inch pieces
- 1 can (about 15 ounces) cannellini beans, rinsed and drained
- 1 turnip, peeled and cut into 1-inch pieces
- 1 large potato, cut into 1-inch pieces
- 2 stalks celery, sliced
- 2 tablespoons minced fresh basil
- 2 teaspoons salt
- 1 teaspoon black pepper

1. Press BROWN/SAUTÉ on **CROCK-POT®** Express Crock Multi-Cooker; heat oil on HIGH. Add beef; cook and stir 6 to 8 minutes or until browned on all sides. Add onion and garlic during last few minutes of browning. Add water, tomatoes, squash, beans, turnip, potato, celery, basil, salt and pepper; stir to blend. Secure lid. Press SOUP, set pressure to HIGH and time to 10 minutes. Make sure Steam Release Valve is in the "Seal" (closed) position. Press START/STOP.

2. Once cooking is complete, quick release pressure. Serve in individual bowls.

SLOW

- 2 tablespoons olive oil
- 1 pound cubed beef stew meat
- 1 medium onion, chopped
- 1 clove garlic, minced
- 6 cups water
- 3½ cups canned crushed tomatoes, undrained
- 1 butternut squash, cut into 1-inch pieces
- 1 can (about 15 ounces) cannellini beans, rinsed and drained
- 1 turnip, peeled and cut into 1-inch pieces
- 1 large potato, cut into 1-inch pieces
- 2 stalks celery, sliced
- 2 tablespoons minced fresh basil
- 2 teaspoons salt
- 1 teaspoon black pepper

1. Press BROWN/SAUTÉ on **CROCK-POT®** Express Crock Multi-Cooker; heat oil on HIGH. Add beef; cook and stir 6 to 8 minutes or until browned on all sides. Add onion and garlic during last few minutes of browning. Add water, tomatoes, squash, beans, turnip, potato, celery, basil, salt and pepper; stir to blend. Secure lid. Press SLOW COOK, set temperature to LOW and time to 4 to 6 hours. Make sure Steam Release Valve is in the "Release" (open) position. Press START/STOP.

2. Once cooking is complete, ladle into individual bowls to serve.

GREEK LEMON AND RICE SOUP

MAKES 4 SERVINGS

3 cans (about 14 ounces *each*) chicken broth

½ cup uncooked long grain rice

3 egg yolks

¼ cup fresh lemon juice

Salt and black pepper

4 thin slices lemon (optional)

4 teaspoons finely chopped fresh oregano (optional)

1. Combine broth and rice in **CROCK-POT®** Express Crock Multi-Cooker. Secure lid. Press RICE/RISOTTO, set pressure to LOW and time to 12 minutes. Make sure Steam Release Valve is in the "Seal" (closed) position. Press START/STOP.

2. Once cooking is complete, quick release pressure. Whisk together egg yolks and lemon juice in medium bowl. Add large spoonful of hot rice mixture to egg yolk mixture; whisk mixture back into remaining rice mixture. Season with salt and pepper. Garnish with lemon slices and oregano.

3 cans (about 14 ounces *each*) chicken broth

½ cup uncooked long grain rice

3 egg yolks

¼ cup fresh lemon juice

Salt and black pepper

4 thin slices lemon (optional)

4 teaspoons finely chopped fresh oregano (optional)

1. Combine broth and rice in **CROCK-POT®** Express Crock Multi-Cooker. Secure lid. Press SLOW COOK, set temperature to HIGH and time to 2 to 3 hours. Make sure Steam Release Valve is in the "Release" (open) position. Press START/STOP.

2. Once cooking is complete, whisk together egg yolks and lemon juice in medium bowl. Add large spoonful of hot rice mixture to egg yolk mixture; whisk mixture back into remaining rice mixture. Season with salt and pepper. Garnish with lemon slices and oregano.

ROASTED CORN AND RED PEPPER CHOWDER

MAKES 4 SERVINGS

FAST

2 tablespoons extra virgin olive oil

2 cups fresh corn

1 red bell pepper, diced

2 green onions, sliced

4 cups chicken broth

2 baking potatoes, diced

2 teaspoons salt

1 teaspoon black pepper

1 can (13½ ounces) evaporated milk

2 tablespoons minced fresh Italian parsley (optional)

1. Press BROWN/SAUTÉ on **CROCK-POT®** Express Crock Multi-Cooker; heat oil on HIGH. Add corn, bell pepper and green onions; cook and stir 8 minutes or until vegetables are tender and lightly browned. Add broth, potatoes, salt and black pepper; stir to blend. Secure lid. Press SOUP, set pressure to HIGH and time to 5 minutes. Make sure Steam Release Valve is in the "Seal" (closed) position. Press START/STOP.

2. Once cooking is complete, quick release pressure. Press BROWN/SAUTÉ on Express Crock. Add evaporated milk; cook and stir on HIGH 3 minutes or until heated through. Garnish each serving with parsley.

SLOW

2 tablespoons extra virgin olive oil

2 cups fresh corn

1 red bell pepper, diced

2 green onions, sliced

4 cups chicken broth

2 baking potatoes, diced

2 teaspoons salt

1 teaspoon black pepper

1 can (13½ ounces) evaporated milk

2 tablespoons minced fresh Italian parsley (optional)

1. Press BROWN/SAUTÉ on **CROCK-POT®** Express Crock Multi-Cooker; heat oil on HIGH. Add corn, bell pepper and green onions; cook and stir 8 minutes or until vegetables are tender and lightly browned. Add broth, potatoes, salt and black pepper; stir to blend. Secure lid. Press SLOW COOK, set temperature and time to LOW 7 to 9 hours or to HIGH 4 to 5 hours. Make sure Steam Release Valve is in the "Release" (open) position. Press START/STOP.

2. Once cooking is complete, press BROWN/SAUTÉ on Express Crock. Add evaporated milk; cook and stir on HIGH 3 minutes or until heated through. Garnish each serving with parsley.

Weeknight Beef Stew (*page 88*)

CHILI AND STEW

SAVORY CHICKEN AND OREGANO CHILI

MAKES 8 SERVINGS

FAST

3 cans (about 15 ounces *each*) cannellini beans, rinsed and drained

3 cups chicken broth

2 boneless, skinless chicken breasts

2 medium red bell peppers, chopped

1 medium onion, chopped

1 can (4 ounces) diced mild green chiles, drained

3 cloves garlic, minced

2 teaspoons ground cumin

1 teaspoon salt

1 tablespoon minced fresh oregano (optional)

1. Combine beans, broth, chicken, bell peppers, onion, chiles, garlic, cumin and salt in **CROCK-POT®** Express Crock Multi-Cooker; stir to blend. Secure lid. Press SOUP, set pressure to HIGH and time to 15 minutes. Make sure Steam Release Valve is in the "Seal" (closed) position. Press START/STOP.

2. Once cooking is complete, natural release pressure 10 minutes. Release remaining pressure. Remove chicken to large cutting board; shred with two forks. Stir shredded chicken back into Express Crock. Garnish each serving with oregano.

SLOW

3 cans (about 15 ounces *each*) cannellini beans, rinsed and drained

3 cups chicken broth

2 boneless, skinless chicken breasts

2 medium red bell peppers, chopped

1 medium onion, chopped

1 can (4 ounces) diced mild green chiles, drained

3 cloves garlic, minced

2 teaspoons ground cumin

1 teaspoon salt

1 tablespoon minced fresh oregano (optional)

1. Combine beans, broth, chicken, bell peppers, onion, chiles, garlic, cumin and salt in **CROCK-POT®** Express Crock Multi-Cooker; stir to blend. Secure lid. Press SLOW COOK, set temperature and time to LOW 8 to 10 hours or to HIGH 4 to 5 hours. Make sure Steam Release Valve is in the "Release" (open) position. Press START/STOP.

2. Once cooking is complete, remove chicken to large cutting board; shred with two forks. Stir shredded chicken back into Express Crock. Garnish each serving with oregano.

STEW PROVENÇAL

MAKES 8 SERVINGS

FAST

- 1 to 2 pork tenderloins (about 2 pounds), trimmed and cut into 1-inch pieces
- 3 tablespoons all-purpose flour
- 1 teaspoon salt
- 1 teaspoon dried thyme
- 1/2 teaspoon black pepper
- 2 tablespoons olive oil
- 2 cups beef broth
- 4 red potatoes, unpeeled and cut into cubes
- 2 cups frozen cut green beans, thawed
- 1 onion, chopped
- 2 cloves garlic, minced
- Sprigs fresh thyme (optional)

1. Place pork, flour, salt, dried thyme and pepper in large resealable food storage bag; toss to coat. Press BROWN/SAUTÉ on **CROCK-POT®** Express Crock Multi-Cooker; heat oil on HIGH. Add pork mixture; cook, uncovered, 5 minutes or until browned. Add broth, potatoes, beans, onion and garlic; stir to blend. Secure lid. Press MEAT/STEW, set pressure to HIGH and time to 15 minutes. Make sure Steam Release Valve is in the "Seal" (closed) position. Press START/STOP.

2. Once cooking is complete, quick release pressure. Garnish each serving with thyme sprigs.

SLOW

- 1 to 2 pork tenderloins (about 2 pounds), trimmed and cut into 1-inch pieces
- 3 tablespoons all-purpose flour
- 1 teaspoon salt
- 1 teaspoon dried thyme
- 1/2 teaspoon black pepper
- 2 tablespoons olive oil
- 2 cups beef broth
- 4 red potatoes, unpeeled and cut into cubes
- 2 cups frozen cut green beans, thawed
- 1 onion, chopped
- 2 cloves garlic, minced
- Sprigs fresh thyme (optional)

1. Place pork, flour, salt, dried thyme and pepper in large resealable food storage bag; toss to coat. Press BROWN/SAUTÉ on **CROCK-POT®** Express Crock Multi-Cooker; heat oil on HIGH. Add pork mixture; cook, uncovered, 5 minutes or until browned. Add broth, potatoes, beans, onion and garlic; stir to blend. Secure lid. Press SLOW COOK, set temperature and time to LOW 8 to 10 hours or to HIGH 4 to 5 hours. Make sure Steam Release Valve is in the "Release" (open) position. Press START/STOP.

2. Once cooking is complete, garnish each serving with thyme sprigs.

HEARTY LENTIL STEW

MAKES 6 SERVINGS

FAST

2 cups cauliflower florets

1 package (16 ounces) frozen green beans

2 cups vegetable broth

1 can (15 ounces) chunky tomato sauce with garlic and herbs

1 cup dried lentils, rinsed and sorted

1 cup chopped onion

1 cup baby carrots

2 teaspoons ground cumin

$3/4$ teaspoon ground ginger

$1/2$ cup peanuts (optional)

1. Combine cauliflower, beans, broth, tomato sauce, lentils, onion, carrots, cumin and ginger in **CROCK-POT®** Express Crock Multi-Cooker; stir to blend. Secure lid. Press BEANS/CHILI, set pressure to HIGH and time to 8 minutes. Make sure Steam Release Valve is in the "Seal" (closed) position. Press START/STOP.

2. Once cooking is complete, natural release pressure 10 minutes. Release remaining pressure. Sprinkle each serving evenly with peanuts, if desired.

SLOW

2 cups cauliflower florets

1 package (16 ounces) frozen green beans

3 cups vegetable broth

1 can (15 ounces) chunky tomato sauce with garlic and herbs

1 cup dried lentils, rinsed and sorted

1 cup chopped onion

1 cup baby carrots

2 teaspoons ground cumin

$3/4$ teaspoon ground ginger

$1/2$ cup peanuts (optional)

1. Combine cauliflower, beans, broth, tomato sauce, lentils, onion, carrots, cumin and ginger in **CROCK-POT®** Express Crock Multi-Cooker; stir to blend. Secure lid. Press SLOW COOK, set temperature to LOW and time to 9 hours. Make sure Steam Release Valve is in the "Release" (open) position. Press START/STOP.

2. Once cooking is complete, sprinkle each serving evenly with peanuts, if desired.

CHICKEN AND MUSHROOM STEW

MAKES 6 SERVINGS

4 tablespoons vegetable oil, divided

6 boneless, skinless chicken thighs (about 2 pounds)

Salt and black pepper

2 medium leeks (white and light green parts only), halved lengthwise and thinly sliced crosswise

12 ounces cremini mushrooms, quartered

1 carrot, cut into 1-inch pieces

1 stalk celery, diced

1 ounce dried porcini mushrooms, rehydrated in 1 1/2 cups hot water and chopped, soaking liquid strained and reserved

1 teaspoon minced garlic

1 sprig fresh thyme

1 whole bay leaf

1/4 cup all-purpose flour

1/2 cup dry white wine

1 cup chicken broth

1. Press BROWN/SAUTÉ on **CROCK-POT®** Express Crock Multi-Cooker; heat 1 tablespoon oil on HIGH. Season chicken with salt and pepper. Add chicken to Express Crock; cook chicken in batches 5 to 7 minutes or until browned. Repeat with 1 tablespoon oil and chicken. Remove to large plate.

2. Heat 1 tablespoon oil in Express Crock. Add leeks; cook 8 minutes or until softened. Add remaining 1 tablespoon oil, cremini mushrooms, carrot and celery; cook 7 minutes or until mushrooms have released their liquid and started to brown. Add porcini mushrooms, garlic, thyme, bay leaf and flour; cook and stir 1 minute. Add wine; cook and stir until evaporated, scraping up any browned bits from bottom of Express Crock.

3. Add chicken, reserved soaking liquid and broth. Secure lid. Press POULTRY, set pressure to HIGH and time to 15 minutes. Make sure Steam Release Valve is in the "Seal" (closed) position. Press START/STOP.

4. Once cooking is complete, quick release pressure. Remove and discard thyme sprig and bay leaf before serving.

4 tablespoons vegetable oil, divided

6 boneless, skinless chicken thighs (about 2 pounds)

Salt and black pepper

2 medium leeks (white and light green parts only), halved lengthwise and thinly sliced crosswise

12 ounces cremini mushrooms, quartered

1 carrot, cut into 1-inch pieces

1 stalk celery, diced

1 ounce dried porcini mushrooms, rehydrated in 1 1/2 cups hot water and chopped, soaking liquid strained and reserved

1 teaspoon minced garlic

1 sprig fresh thyme

1 whole bay leaf

1/4 cup all-purpose flour

1/2 cup dry white wine

1 cup chicken broth

1. Press BROWN/SAUTÉ on **CROCK-POT®** Express Crock Multi-Cooker; heat 1 tablespoon oil on HIGH. Season chicken with salt and pepper. Add chicken to Express Crock; cook chicken in batches 5 to 7 minutes or until browned. Repeat with 1 tablespoon oil and chicken. Remove to large plate.

2. Heat 1 tablespoon oil in Express Crock. Add leeks; cook 8 minutes or until softened. Add remaining 1 tablespoon oil, cremini mushrooms, carrot and celery; cook 7 minutes or until mushrooms have released their liquid and started to brown. Add porcini mushrooms, garlic, thyme, bay leaf and flour; cook and stir 1 minute. Add wine; cook and stir until evaporated, scraping up any browned bits from bottom of Express Crock.

3. Add chicken, reserved soaking liquid and broth. Secure lid. Press SLOW COOK, set temperature to HIGH and time to 2 to 3 hours. Make sure Steam Release Valve is in the "Release" (open) position. Press START/STOP.

4. Once cooking is complete, remove and discard thyme sprig and bay leaf before serving.

CHIPOTLE VEGETABLE CHILI WITH CHOCOLATE

MAKES 6 SERVINGS

FAST

- 2 tablespoons olive oil
- 1 medium onion, chopped
- 1 medium green bell pepper, chopped
- 1 medium red bell pepper, chopped
- 1 cup frozen corn
- 1 can (28 ounces) diced tomatoes
- 1 can (about 15 ounces) black beans, rinsed and drained
- 1 can (about 15 ounces) pinto beans, rinsed and drained
- 1 tablespoon chili powder
- 1 teaspoon ground cumin
- 1/2 teaspoon chipotle chili powder
- 1 ounce semisweet chocolate, chopped

1. Press BROWN/SAUTÉ on **CROCK-POT®** Express Crock Multi-Cooker; heat oil on HIGH. Add onion and bell peppers; cook and stir 4 minutes or until softened. Stir in corn; cook 3 minutes. Stir tomatoes, beans, chili powder, cumin and chipotle chili powder into Express Crock. Secure lid. Press BEANS/CHILI, set pressure to HIGH and time to 7 minutes. Make sure Steam Release Valve is in the "Seal" (closed) position. Press START/STOP.

2. Once cooking is complete, natural release pressure 10 minutes. Release remaining pressure. Stir chocolate into Express Crock until melted.

SLOW

- 2 tablespoons olive oil
- 1 medium onion, chopped
- 1 medium green bell pepper, chopped
- 1 medium red bell pepper, chopped
- 1 cup frozen corn
- 1 can (28 ounces) diced tomatoes
- 1 can (about 15 ounces) black beans, rinsed and drained
- 1 can (about 15 ounces) pinto beans, rinsed and drained
- 1 tablespoon chili powder
- 1 teaspoon ground cumin
- 1/2 teaspoon chipotle chili powder
- 1 ounce semisweet chocolate, chopped

1. Press BROWN/SAUTÉ on **CROCK-POT®** Express Crock Multi-Cooker; heat oil on HIGH. Add onion and bell peppers; cook and stir 4 minutes or until softened. Stir in corn; cook 3 minutes. Stir tomatoes, beans, chili powder, cumin and chipotle chili powder into Express Crock. Press SLOW COOK, set temperature to LOW and time to 6 to 7 hours. Make sure Steam Release Valve is in the "Release" (open) position. Press START/STOP.

2. Once cooking is complete, stir chocolate into Express Crock until melted.

CORN CHIP CHILI

MAKES 6 SERVINGS

2 pounds ground beef

1 tablespoon olive oil

1 medium onion, chopped

1 medium red bell pepper, chopped

1 jalapeño pepper, seeded and finely chopped*

4 cloves garlic, minced

1 can (4 ounces) diced mild green chiles, drained

2 cans (about 14 ounces each) fire-roasted diced tomatoes

2 tablespoons chili powder

1 1/2 teaspoons ground cumin

1 1/2 teaspoons dried oregano

3/4 teaspoon salt

3 cups corn chips

1 cup (4 ounces) shredded sharp Cheddar cheese

6 tablespoons chopped green onions

Jalapeño peppers can sting and irritate the skin, so wear rubber gloves when handling peppers and do not touch your eyes.

1. Press BROWN/SAUTÉ on **CROCK-POT®** Express Crock Multi-Cooker. Add beef; cook and stir 6 to 8 minutes or until browned, stirring to break up meat. Drain fat. Remove beef to large bowl. Wipe Express Crock clean.

2. Heat oil on HIGH. Add onion, bell pepper, jalapeño pepper and garlic; cook and stir 2 minutes or until softened. Stir in green chiles; cook 1 minute. Stir in tomatoes, chili powder, cumin, oregano and salt. Secure lid. Press BEANS/CHILI, set pressure to HIGH and time to 10 minutes. Make sure Steam Release Valve is in the "Seal" (closed) position. Press START/STOP.

3. Once cooking is complete, natural release pressure 10 minutes. Release remaining pressure. Place corn chips evenly into serving bowls; top with chili. Sprinkle evenly with cheese and green onions.

2 pounds ground beef

1 tablespoon olive oil

1 medium onion, chopped

1 medium red bell pepper, chopped

1 jalapeño pepper, seeded and finely chopped*

4 cloves garlic, minced

1 can (4 ounces) diced mild green chiles, drained

2 cans (about 14 ounces each) fire-roasted diced tomatoes

2 tablespoons chili powder

1 1/2 teaspoons ground cumin

1 1/2 teaspoons dried oregano

3/4 teaspoon salt

3 cups corn chips

1 cup (4 ounces) shredded sharp Cheddar cheese

6 tablespoons chopped green onions

Jalapeño peppers can sting and irritate the skin, so wear rubber gloves when handling peppers and do not touch your eyes.

1. Press BROWN/SAUTÉ on **CROCK-POT®** Express Crock Multi-Cooker. Add beef; cook and stir 6 to 8 minutes or until browned, stirring to break up meat. Drain fat. Remove beef to large bowl. Wipe Express Crock clean.

2. Heat oil on HIGH. Add onion, bell pepper, jalapeño pepper and garlic; cook and stir 2 minutes or until softened. Stir in green chiles; cook 1 minute. Stir in tomatoes, chili powder, cumin, oregano and salt. Secure lid. Press SLOW COOK, set temperature and time to LOW 6 to 7 hours or to HIGH 3 to 4 hours. Make sure Steam Release Valve is in the "Release" (open) position. Press START/STOP.

3. Once cooking is complete, place corn chips evenly into serving bowls. Top with chili; sprinkle evenly with cheese and green onions.

THREE-BEAN TURKEY CHILI

MAKES 6 TO 8 SERVINGS

FAST

- 1 **pound ground turkey**
- 1 **small onion, chopped**
- 1 **can (28 ounces) diced tomatoes**
- 1 **can (about 15 ounces) chickpeas, rinsed and drained**
- 1 **can (about 15 ounces) kidney beans, rinsed and drained**
- 1 **can (about 15 ounces) black beans, rinsed and drained**
- 1 **can (8 ounces) tomato sauce**
- 1 **can (4 ounces) diced mild green chiles**
- 1 **to 2 tablespoons chili powder**
- 1 **teaspoon salt**

1. Press BROWN/SAUTÉ on **CROCK-POT®** Express Crock Multi-Cooker. Add turkey and onion; cook and stir on HIGH 8 minutes or until turkey is browned. Add tomatoes, chickpeas, beans, tomato sauce, chiles, chili powder and salt to Express Crock; stir to blend. Secure lid. Press BEANS/CHILI, set pressure to HIGH and time to 10 minutes. Make sure Steam Release Valve is in the "Seal" (closed) position. Press START/STOP.

2. Once cooking is complete, natural release pressure 10 minutes. Release remaining pressure. Adjust seasonings, if desired.

SLOW

- 1 **pound ground turkey**
- 1 **small onion, chopped**
- 1 **can (28 ounces) diced tomatoes**
- 1 **can (about 15 ounces) chickpeas, rinsed and drained**
- 1 **can (about 15 ounces) kidney beans, rinsed and drained**
- 1 **can (about 15 ounces) black beans, rinsed and drained**
- 1 **can (8 ounces) tomato sauce**
- 1 **can (4 ounces) diced mild green chiles**
- 1 **to 2 tablespoons chili powder**
- 1 **teaspoon salt**

1. Press BROWN/SAUTÉ on **CROCK-POT®** Express Crock Multi-Cooker. Add turkey and onion; cook and stir on HIGH 8 minutes or until turkey is browned. Add tomatoes, chickpeas, beans, tomato sauce, chiles, chili powder and salt to Express Crock; stir to blend. Secure lid. Press SLOW COOK, set temperature to HIGH and time to 6 to 8 hours. Make sure Steam Release Valve is in the "Release" (open) position. Press START/STOP.

2. Once cooking is complete, adjust seasonings, if desired.

BEEF STEW WITH MOLASSES AND RAISINS

MAKES 6 TO 8 SERVINGS

FAST

- 1/3 cup all-purpose flour
- 2 teaspoons salt, divided
- 1 1/2 teaspoons black pepper, divided
- 2 pounds boneless beef chuck roast, cut into 1 1/2-inch pieces
- 5 tablespoons olive oil, divided
- 2 medium onions, sliced
- 1 can (28 ounces) diced tomatoes, drained
- 1 small package (8 ounces) baby carrots, cut into halves lengthwise
- 2 parsnips, diced
- 1 cup beef broth
- 1/2 cup golden raisins
- 3 tablespoons molasses
- 2 tablespoons cider vinegar
- 4 cloves garlic, minced
- 2 teaspoons dried thyme
- 1 teaspoon celery salt
- 1 whole bay leaf

1. Combine flour, 1 1/2 teaspoons salt and 1 teaspoon pepper in large resealable food storage bag. Add beef; toss to coat. Press BROWN/SAUTÉ on **CROCK-POT®** Express Crock Multi-Cooker; heat 2 tablespoons oil on HIGH. Add beef in batches; cook, uncovered, 8 minutes or until browned on all sides. Remove to large plate. Repeat with 2 tablespoons oil and remaining beef.

2. Add remaining 1 tablespoon oil to Express Crock. Add onions; cook and stir 5 minutes, scraping up any browned bits from bottom of Express Crock. Add beef, tomatoes, carrots, parsnips, broth, raisins, molasses, vinegar, garlic, thyme, celery salt, bay leaf and remaining 1/2 teaspoon salt and 1/2 teaspoon pepper to Express Crock. Secure lid. Press MEAT/STEW, set pressure to HIGH and time to 25 minutes. Make sure Steam Release Valve is in the "Seal" (closed) position. Press START/STOP.

3. Once cooking is complete, quick release pressure. Remove and discard bay leaf.

SLOW

- 1/3 cup all-purpose flour
- 2 teaspoons salt, divided
- 1 1/2 teaspoons black pepper, divided
- 2 pounds boneless beef chuck roast, cut into 1 1/2-inch pieces
- 5 tablespoons olive oil, divided
- 2 medium onions, sliced
- 1 can (28 ounces) diced tomatoes, drained
- 1 cup beef broth
- 3 tablespoons molasses
- 2 tablespoons cider vinegar
- 4 cloves garlic, minced
- 2 teaspoons dried thyme
- 1 teaspoon celery salt
- 1 whole bay leaf
- 1 small package (8 ounces) baby carrots, cut into halves lengthwise
- 2 parsnips, diced
- 1/2 cup golden raisins

1. Combine flour, 1 1/2 teaspoons salt and 1 teaspoon pepper in large resealable food storage bag. Add beef; toss to coat. Press BROWN/SAUTÉ on **CROCK-POT®** Express Crock Multi-Cooker; heat 2 tablespoons oil on HIGH. Add half of beef; cook 8 minutes or until browned on all sides. Remove to large plate. Repeat with 2 tablespoons oil and remaining beef.

2. Add remaining 1 tablespoon oil to Express Crock. Add onions; cook and stir 5 minutes, scraping up any browned bits from bottom of Express Crock. Add beef, tomatoes, broth, molasses, vinegar, garlic, thyme,

celery salt, bay leaf and remaining ½ teaspoon salt and ½ teaspoon pepper to Express Crock. Secure lid. Press SLOW COOK, set temperature and time to LOW 5 hours or to HIGH 2½ hours. Make sure Steam Release Valve is in the "Release" (open) position. Press START/STOP.

3. Once cooking is complete, remove lid and add carrots, parsnips and raisins. Secure lid. Press SLOW COOK, set temperature and time to LOW 2 hours or to HIGH 1 hour. Make sure Steam Release Valve is in the "Release" (open) position. Press START/STOP.

4. Once cooking is complete, remove and discard bay leaf.

SPICY CHICKEN CHILI

MAKES 6 SERVINGS

FAST

2 cans (about 15 ounces *each*) cannellini or small white beans, rinsed and drained

1 can (about 14 ounces) chicken broth

2 onions, chopped

1 can (about 14 ounces) cream-style corn

1 red bell pepper, chopped

3 cloves garlic, minced

2 jalapeño peppers, seeded and chopped*

2 tablespoons chili powder

2 teaspoons ground cumin

3 boneless, skinless chicken thighs

3/4 teaspoon ground red pepper

3/4 teaspoon salt

1/2 teaspoon black pepper

Optional toppings: sour cream, tortilla strips and fresh cilantro leaves (optional)

Jalapeño peppers can sting and irritate the skin, so wear rubber gloves when handling peppers and do not touch your eyes.

1. Combine beans, broth, onions, corn, bell pepper, garlic, jalapeño peppers, chili powder and cumin in **CROCK-POT®** Express Crock Multi-Cooker; stir to blend. Add chicken. Secure lid. Press BEANS/CHILI, set pressure to HIGH and time to 15 minutes. Make sure Steam Release Valve is in the "Seal" (closed) position. Press START/STOP.

2. Once cooking is complete, natural release pressure 10 minutes. Remove chicken to large cutting board; shred with two forks. Add ground red pepper, salt and black pepper to Express Crock; mash chili. Stir shredded chicken back into Express Crock. Top each serving as desired.

SLOW

2 cans (about 15 ounces *each*) cannellini or small white beans, rinsed and drained

1 can (about 14 ounces) chicken broth

2 onions, chopped

1 can (about 14 ounces) cream-style corn

1 red bell pepper, chopped

3 cloves garlic, minced

2 jalapeño peppers, seeded and chopped*

2 tablespoons chili powder

2 teaspoons ground cumin

3 boneless, skinless chicken thighs

3/4 teaspoon ground red pepper

3/4 teaspoon salt

1/2 teaspoon black pepper

Optional toppings: sour cream, tortilla strips and fresh cilantro leaves (optional)

Jalapeño peppers can sting and irritate the skin, so wear rubber gloves when handling peppers and do not touch your eyes.

1. Combine beans, broth, onions, corn, bell pepper, garlic, jalapeño peppers, chili powder and cumin in **CROCK-POT®** Express Crock Multi-Cooker; stir to blend. Add chicken. Secure lid. Press SLOW COOK, set temperature and time to LOW 7 to 8 hours or to HIGH 3 to 4 hours. Make sure Steam Release Valve is in the "Release" (open) position. Press START/STOP.

2. Once cooking is complete, remove chicken to large cutting board and shred with two forks. Add ground red pepper, salt and black pepper to Express Crock; mash chili. Stir shredded chicken back into Express Crock. Top each serving as desired.

SWEET AND SOUR BRISKET STEW

MAKES 6 TO 8 SERVINGS

FAST

- 1 jar (12 ounces) sweet chili sauce
- 1½ tablespoons packed dark brown sugar
- 1½ tablespoons lemon juice
- ¼ cup beef broth
- 1 tablespoon Dijon mustard
- ¼ teaspoon paprika
- ½ teaspoon salt
- ¼ teaspoon black pepper
- 1 beef brisket, trimmed and cut into 1-inch cubes*
- 2 carrots, cut into ½-inch slices
- 1 medium onion, chopped
- 1 clove garlic, minced
- 1 tablespoon all-purpose flour

Beef brisket has a thick layer of fat, which some supermarkets trim off. If the meat is well trimmed, buy 2½ pounds; if not, purchase 4 pounds, then trim and discard excess fat.

1. Combine chili sauce, brown sugar, lemon juice, broth, mustard, paprika, salt and pepper in **CROCK-POT®** Express Crock Multi-Cooker; stir to blend. Add beef, carrots, onion and garlic; toss to coat beef. Secure lid. Press MEAT/STEW, set pressure to HIGH and time to 20 minutes. Make sure Steam Release Valve is in the "Seal" (closed) position. Press START/STOP.

2. Once cooking is complete, natural release pressure 10 minutes. Release remaining pressure. Press BROWN/SAUTÉ on Express Crock. Stir 3 tablespoons cooking liquid into flour in small bowl until smooth. Stir into Express Crock; cook and stir on HIGH 5 to 10 minutes or until thickened.

SLOW

- 1 jar (12 ounces) sweet chili sauce
- 1½ tablespoons packed dark brown sugar
- 1½ tablespoons lemon juice
- ¼ cup beef broth
- 1 tablespoon Dijon mustard
- ¼ teaspoon paprika
- ½ teaspoon salt
- ¼ teaspoon black pepper
- 1 beef brisket, trimmed and cut into 1-inch cubes*
- 2 carrots, cut into ½-inch slices
- 1 medium onion, chopped
- 1 clove garlic, minced
- 1 tablespoon all-purpose flour

Beef brisket has a thick layer of fat, which some supermarkets trim off. If the meat is well trimmed, buy 2½ pounds; if not, purchase 4 pounds, then trim and discard excess fat.

1. Combine chili sauce, brown sugar, lemon juice, broth, mustard, paprika, salt and pepper in **CROCK-POT®** Express Crock Multi-Cooker; stir to blend. Add beef, carrots, onion and garlic; toss to coat beef. Secure lid. Press SLOW COOK, set temperature to LOW and time to 8 hours. Make sure Steam Release Valve is in the "Release" (open) position. Press START/STOP.

2. Once cooking is complete, press BROWN/SAUTÉ on Express Crock. Stir 3 tablespoons cooking liquid into flour in small bowl until smooth. Stir into Express Crock; cook and stir on HIGH 5 to 10 minutes or until thickened.

SUMMER VEGETABLE STEW

MAKES 4 SERVINGS

FAST

- 1 cup vegetable broth
- 1 can (about 15 ounces) chickpeas, rinsed and drained
- 1 medium zucchini, cut into 1/2-inch pieces
- 1 summer squash, cut into 1/2-inch pieces
- 4 large plum tomatoes, cut into 1/2-inch pieces
- 1 cup frozen corn
- 1 teaspoon minced garlic
- 1/2 to 1 teaspoon dried rosemary
- 1/4 cup grated Asiago or Parmesan cheese
- 1 tablespoon chopped fresh Italian parsley

Salt and black pepper

1. Combine broth, chickpeas, zucchini, squash, tomatoes, corn, garlic and rosemary in **CROCK-POT®** Express Crock Multi-Cooker; stir to blend. Secure lid. Press STEAM, set pressure to HIGH and time to 5 minutes. Make sure Steam Release Valve is in the "Seal" (closed) position. Press START/STOP.

2. Once cooking is complete, quick release pressure. Top each serving evenly with cheese and parsley. Season with salt and pepper.

SLOW

- 1 cup vegetable broth
- 1 can (about 15 ounces) chickpeas, rinsed and drained
- 1 medium zucchini, cut into 1/2-inch pieces
- 1 summer squash, cut into 1/2-inch pieces
- 4 large plum tomatoes, cut into 1/2-inch pieces
- 1 cup frozen corn
- 1 teaspoon minced garlic
- 1/2 to 1 teaspoon dried rosemary
- 1/4 cup grated Asiago or Parmesan cheese
- 1 tablespoon chopped fresh Italian parsley

Salt and black pepper

1. Combine broth, chickpeas, zucchini, squash, tomatoes, corn, garlic and rosemary in **CROCK-POT®** Express Crock Multi-Cooker; stir to blend. Secure lid. Press SLOW COOK, set temperature and time to LOW 8 hours or to HIGH 5 hours. Make sure Steam Release Valve is in the "Release" (open) position. Press START/STOP.

2. Once cooking is complete, top each serving evenly with cheese and parsley. Season with salt and pepper.

BLACK AND WHITE CHILI

MAKES 6 SERVINGS

FAST

1 tablespoon vegetable oil

1 cup chopped onion

1 pound boneless, skinless chicken breasts, cut into ¾-inch pieces

1 can (about 15 ounces) cannellini beans, rinsed and drained

1 can (about 15 ounces) black beans, rinsed and drained

1 can (about 14 ounces) stewed tomatoes

1 cup chicken broth

1 package (1¼ ounces) Texas-style chili seasoning mix

1. Press BROWN/SAUTÉ on **CROCK-POT®** Express Crock Multi-Cooker; heat oil on HIGH. Add onion; cook and stir 3 minutes or until softened. Stir in chicken, beans, tomatoes, broth and seasoning mix until well blended. Secure lid. Press BEANS/CHILI, set pressure to HIGH and time to 7 minutes. Make sure Steam Release Valve is in the "Seal" (closed) position. Press START/STOP.

2. Once cooking is complete, natural release pressure 10 minutes. Release remaining pressure. Press BROWN/SAUTÉ on Express Crock; cook and stir 3 to 5 minutes or until desired thickness is reached.

SLOW

1 tablespoon vegetable oil

1 cup chopped onion

1 pound boneless, skinless chicken breasts, cut into ¾-inch pieces

1 can (about 15 ounces) cannellini beans, rinsed and drained

1 can (about 15 ounces) black beans, rinsed and drained

1 can (about 14 ounces) stewed tomatoes

2 tablespoons Texas-style chili seasoning mix

1. Press BROWN/SAUTÉ on **CROCK-POT®** Express Crock Multi-Cooker; heat oil on HIGH. Add onion; cook and stir 3 minutes or until softened. Stir in chicken, beans, tomatoes and seasoning mix until well blended. Secure lid. Press SLOW COOK, set temperature to LOW and time to 4 to 4½ hours. Make sure Steam Release Valve is in the "Release" (open) position. Press START/STOP.

2. Once cooking is complete, press BROWN/SAUTÉ on Express Crock; cook and stir chili on HIGH 3 to 5 minutes or until desired thickness is reached.

CINCINNATI CHILI

MAKES 6 SERVINGS

1 tablespoon vegetable oil

2 medium onions, chopped

2 pounds ground beef

1 can (28 ounces) diced tomatoes

1 cup tomato sauce

½ cup water

3 cloves garlic, minced

1 tablespoon unsweetened cocoa powder

1 tablespoon chili powder

2½ teaspoons ground cinnamon

2 teaspoons salt

1½ teaspoons ground cumin

1½ teaspoons Worcestershire sauce

1¼ teaspoons ground allspice

¾ teaspoon ground red pepper

12 ounces cooked spaghetti

Optional toppings: chopped onions, shredded Cheddar cheese, kidney beans and/or oyster crackers

1. Press BROWN/SAUTÉ on **CROCK-POT®** Express Crock Multi-Cooker; heat oil on HIGH. Add onions; cook 2 to 3 minutes. Add beef; cook 6 to 8 minutes or until beef is browned, stirring to break up meat. Drain fat.

2. Stir tomatoes, tomato sauce, water, garlic, cocoa, chili powder, cinnamon, salt, cumin, Worcestershire sauce, allspice and ground red pepper into Express Crock. Secure lid. Press BEANS/CHILI, set pressure to HIGH and time to 10 minutes. Make sure Steam Release Valve is in the "Seal" (closed) position. Press START/STOP.

3. Once cooking is complete, natural release pressure 10 minutes. Release remaining pressure. Spoon chili over spaghetti. Top as desired.

1 tablespoon vegetable oil

2 medium onions, chopped

2 pounds ground beef

1 can (28 ounces) diced tomatoes

1 cup tomato sauce

½ cup water

3 cloves garlic, minced

1 tablespoon unsweetened cocoa powder

1 tablespoon chili powder

2½ teaspoons ground cinnamon

2 teaspoons salt

1½ teaspoons ground cumin

1½ teaspoons Worcestershire sauce

1¼ teaspoons ground allspice

¾ teaspoon ground red pepper

12 ounces cooked spaghetti

Optional toppings: chopped onions, shredded Cheddar cheese, kidney beans and/or oyster crackers

1. Press BROWN/SAUTÉ on **CROCK-POT®** Express Crock Multi-Cooker; heat oil on HIGH. Add onions; cook 2 to 3 minutes. Add beef; cook 6 to 8 minutes or until beef is browned, stirring to break up meat. Drain fat.

2. Stir tomatoes, tomato sauce, water, garlic, cocoa, chili powder, cinnamon, salt, cumin, Worcestershire sauce, allspice and ground red pepper into Express Crock. Secure lid. Press SLOW COOK, set temperature and time to LOW 7 to 8 hours or to HIGH 3½ to 4 hours. Make sure Steam Release Valve is in the "Release" (open) position. Press START/STOP.

3. Once cooking is complete, spoon chili over spaghetti. Top as desired.

MEDITERRANEAN CHILI

MAKES 6 SERVINGS

FAST

2 cans (about 28 ounces *each*) chickpeas, rinsed and drained

1 can (28 ounces) diced tomatoes

1 can (about 14 ounces) vegetable broth

2 medium onions, chopped

10 kalamata olives, chopped

4 cloves garlic, chopped

2 teaspoons ground cumin

1 teaspoon dried oregano

1/4 teaspoon ground red pepper

1/2 cup chopped fresh mint

1/2 teaspoon grated lemon peel

1 cup crumbled feta cheese

Sprigs fresh mint (optional)

Olive oil (optional)

Pita bread rounds (optional)

1. Combine chickpeas, tomatoes, broth, onions, olives, garlic, cumin, oregano and ground red pepper in **CROCK-POT** Express Crock Multi-Cooker; stir to blend. Secure lid. Press BEANS/CHILI, set pressure to HIGH and time to 7 minutes. Make sure Steam Release Valve is in the "Seal" (closed) position. Press START/STOP.

2. Once cooking is complete, natural release pressure 10 minutes. Stir in chopped mint and lemon peel; top each serving with feta. Garnish with mint sprigs and drizzle of oil. Serve with pita bread rounds, if desired.

SLOW

2 cans (about 28 ounces *each*) chickpeas, rinsed and drained

1 can (28 ounces) diced tomatoes

1 can (about 14 ounces) vegetable broth

2 medium onions, chopped

10 kalamata olives, chopped

4 cloves garlic, chopped

2 teaspoons ground cumin

1 teaspoon dried oregano

1/4 teaspoon ground red pepper

1/2 cup chopped fresh mint

1/2 teaspoon grated lemon peel

1 cup crumbled feta cheese

Sprigs fresh mint (optional)

Olive oil (optional)

Pita bread rounds (optional)

1. Combine chickpeas, tomatoes, broth, onions, olives, garlic, cumin, oregano and ground red pepper in **CROCK-POT®** Express Crock Multi-Cooker; stir to blend. Secure lid. Press SLOW COOK, set temperature and time to LOW 7 to 8 hours or to HIGH 3 to 4 hours. Make sure Steam Release Valve is in the "Release" (open) position. Press START/STOP.

2. Once cooking is complete, stir in chopped mint and lemon peel. Top each serving with feta. Garnish with mint sprigs and drizzle of oil. Serve with pita bread rounds, if desired.

SWISS STEAK STEW

MAKES 10 SERVINGS

FAST

2 to 3 boneless beef top sirloin steaks (about 4 pounds), cut into 3 to 4 pieces

1 can (about 14 ounces) diced tomatoes

2 medium green bell peppers, cut into ½-inch strips

2 medium onions, coarsely chopped

1 tablespoon seasoned salt

1 teaspoon black pepper

1. Combine steak, tomatoes, bell peppers, onions, seasoned salt and black pepper in **CROCK-POT®** Express Crock Multi-Cooker. Secure lid. Press MEAT/STEW, set pressure to HIGH and time to 20 minutes. Make sure Steam Release Valve is in the "Seal" (closed) position. Press START/STOP.

2. Once cooking is complete, natural release pressure 10 minutes. Release remaining pressure. Adjust seasonings, if desired.

SLOW

2 to 3 boneless beef top sirloin steaks (about 4 pounds), cut into 3 to 4 pieces

1 can (about 14 ounces) diced tomatoes

2 medium green bell peppers, cut into ½-inch strips

2 medium onions, coarsely chopped

1 tablespoon seasoned salt

1 teaspoon black pepper

1. Combine steak, tomatoes, bell peppers, onions, seasoned salt and black pepper in **CROCK-POT®** Express Crock Multi-Cooker. Secure lid. Press SLOW COOK, set temperature to LOW and time to 8 hours. Make sure Steam Release Valve is in the "Release" (open) position. Press START/STOP.

2. Once cooking is complete, adjust seasonings, if desired.

CHICKEN AND SWEET POTATO STEW

MAKES 6 SERVINGS

- 4 boneless, skinless chicken breasts, cut into 1-inch pieces
- 2 medium sweet potatoes, cubed
- 2 medium Yukon Gold potatoes, cubed
- 2 medium carrots, cut into 1/2-inch slices
- 1 can (28 ounces) whole stewed tomatoes
- 1 cup chicken broth
- 1 teaspoon salt
- 1 teaspoon paprika
- 1 teaspoon celery seed
- 1/2 teaspoon black pepper
- 1/8 teaspoon ground cinnamon
- 1/8 teaspoon ground nutmeg
- 1/4 cup fresh basil, chopped

1. Combine chicken, sweet potatoes, Yukon Gold potatoes, carrots, tomatoes, broth, salt, paprika, celery seed, pepper, cinnamon and nutmeg in **CROCK-POT®** Express Crock Multi-Cooker; stir to blend. Secure lid. Press STEAM, set pressure to HIGH and time to 7 minutes. Make sure Steam Release Valve is in the "Seal" (closed) position. Press START/STOP.

2. Once cooking is complete, natural release pressure 10 minutes. Release remaining pressure. Press BROWN/SAUTÉ on Express Crock. Heat stew on HIGH 2 to 3 minutes or until desired thickness. Sprinkle each serving with basil.

- 4 boneless, skinless chicken breasts, cut into 1-inch pieces
- 2 medium sweet potatoes, cubed
- 2 medium Yukon Gold potatoes, cubed
- 2 medium carrots, cut into 1/2-inch slices
- 1 can (28 ounces) whole stewed tomatoes
- 1 cup chicken broth
- 1 teaspoon salt
- 1 teaspoon paprika
- 1 teaspoon celery seed
- 1/2 teaspoon black pepper
- 1/8 teaspoon ground cinnamon
- 1/8 teaspoon ground nutmeg
- 1/4 cup fresh basil, chopped

1. Combine chicken, sweet potatoes, Yukon Gold potatoes, carrots, tomatoes, broth, salt, paprika, celery seed, pepper, cinnamon and nutmeg in **CROCK-POT®** Express Crock Multi-Cooker; stir to blend. Secure lid. Press SLOW COOK, set temperature and time to LOW 6 to 8 hours or to HIGH 3 to 4 hours. Make sure Steam Release Valve is in the "Release" (open) position. Press START/STOP.

2. Once cooking is complete, press BROWN/SAUTÉ on Express Crock. Heat on HIGH 2 to 3 minutes or until desired thickness. Sprinkle each serving with basil.

WEEKNIGHT BEEF STEW

MAKES 6 SERVINGS

1½ **pounds cubed beef stew meat**

5 **tablespoons all-purpose flour, divided**

1 **teaspoon dried thyme**

1 **teaspoon salt**

1 **teaspoon black pepper**

1 **tablespoon olive oil**

2 **medium russet potatoes (about 1 pound), cut into ½-inch pieces**

4 **medium carrots, thickly sliced**

1 **large onion, cut into thin wedges**

2 **cups beef broth, divided**

Chopped fresh thyme (optional)

1. Place beef, 2 tablespoons flour, dried thyme, salt and pepper in large resealable food storage bag; shake to coat. Press BROWN/SAUTÉ on **CROCK-POT®** Express Crock Multi-Cooker; heat oil on HIGH. Add beef in batches; cook and stir 4 to 5 minutes or until browned on all sides.

2. Add potatoes, carrots and onion. Pour 1½ cups broth over beef and vegetables. Secure lid. Press MEAT/STEW, set pressure to HIGH and time to 20 minutes. Make sure Steam Release Valve is in the "Seal" (closed) position. Press START/STOP.

3. Once cooking is complete, natural release pressure 10 minutes. Release remaining pressure. Press BROWN/SAUTÉ on Express Crock. Stir remaining ½ cup broth into remaining 3 tablespoons flour in small bowl until smooth; whisk flour mixture into stew. Cook, uncovered, on HIGH 5 to 10 minutes or until thickened. Garnish each serving with fresh thyme.

1½ **pounds cubed beef stew meat**

5 **tablespoons all-purpose flour, divided**

1 **teaspoon dried thyme**

1 **teaspoon salt**

1 **teaspoon black pepper**

1 **tablespoon olive oil**

2 **medium russet potatoes (about 1 pound), cut into 2-inch pieces**

4 **medium carrots, thickly sliced**

1 **large onion, cut into thin wedges**

3 **cups beef broth, divided**

Chopped fresh thyme (optional)

1. Place beef, 2 tablespoons flour, dried thyme, salt and pepper in large resealable food storage bag; shake to coat. Press BROWN/SAUTÉ on **CROCK-POT®** Express Crock Multi-Cooker; heat oil on HIGH. Add beef in batches; cook and stir 4 to 5 minutes or until browned on all sides.

2. Add potatoes, carrots and onion. Pour 2½ cups broth over beef and vegetables. Secure lid. Press SLOW COOK, set temperature and time to LOW 8 to 9 hours or to HIGH 4 to 5 hours. Make sure Steam Release Valve is in the "Release" (open) position. Press START/STOP.

3. Once cooking is complete and meat and vegetables are fork-tender, press BROWN/SAUTÉ on Express Crock. Stir remaining ½ cup broth into remaining 3 tablespoons flour in small bowl until smooth; whisk flour mixture into stew. Cook, uncovered, on HIGH 5 to 10 minutes or until thickened. Garnish each serving with fresh thyme.

CHIPOTLE CHICKEN STEW

MAKES 6 SERVINGS

FAST

1 pound boneless, skinless chicken thighs, cubed

1 can (about 15 ounces) cannellini beans, rinsed and drained

1 can (about 15 ounces) black beans, rinsed and drained

1 can (about 14 ounces) crushed tomatoes, undrained

1 1/2 cups chicken broth

1/2 cup orange juice

1 medium onion, diced

1 canned chipotle pepper in adobo sauce, minced

1 teaspoon salt

1 teaspoon ground cumin

1 whole bay leaf

Sprigs fresh cilantro (optional)

1. Combine chicken, beans, tomatoes, broth, orange juice, onion, chipotle pepper, salt, cumin and bay leaf in **CROCK-POT®** Express Crock Multi-Cooker. Secure lid. Press BEANS/CHILI, set pressure to HIGH and time to 7 minutes. Make sure Steam Release Valve is in the "Seal" (closed) position. Press START/STOP.

2. Once cooking is complete, natural release pressure 10 minutes. Release remaining pressure. Remove and discard bay leaf. Garnish each serving with cilantro.

SLOW

1 pound boneless, skinless chicken thighs, cubed

1 can (about 15 ounces) cannellini beans, rinsed and drained

1 can (about 15 ounces) black beans, rinsed and drained

1 can (about 14 ounces) crushed tomatoes, undrained

1 1/2 cups chicken broth

1/2 cup orange juice

1 medium onion, diced

1 canned chipotle pepper in adobo sauce, minced

1 teaspoon salt

1 teaspoon ground cumin

1 whole bay leaf

Sprigs fresh cilantro (optional)

1. Combine chicken, beans, tomatoes, broth, orange juice, onion, chipotle pepper, salt, cumin and bay leaf in **CROCK-POT®** Express Crock Multi-Cooker. Secure lid. Press SLOW COOK, set temperature and time to LOW 7 to 8 hours or to HIGH 3 1/2 to 4 hours. Make sure Steam Release Valve is in the "Release" (open) position. Press START/STOP.

2. Once cooking is complete, remove and discard bay leaf. Garnish each serving with cilantro.

SIMPLE BEEF CHILI

MAKES 8 SERVINGS

FAST

3 pounds ground beef

2 cans (about 14 ounces *each*) diced tomatoes

2 cans (about 15 ounces *each*) kidney beans, rinsed and drained

2 cups chopped onions

1 package (10 ounces) frozen corn

1 cup chopped green bell pepper

1 can (8 ounces) tomato sauce

1 cup beef broth

3 tablespoons chili powder

1 teaspoon garlic powder

1/2 teaspoon ground cumin

1/2 teaspoon dried oregano

1. Press BROWN/SAUTÉ on **CROCK-POT®** Express Crock Multi-Cooker. Add beef; cook on HIGH 6 to 8 minutes, stirring to break up meat. Drain fat.

2. Add tomatoes, beans, onions, corn, bell pepper, tomato sauce, broth, chili powder, garlic powder, cumin and oregano to Express Crock. Secure lid. Press BEANS/CHILI, set pressure to HIGH and time to 10 minutes. Make sure Steam Release Valve is in the "Seal" (closed) position. Press START/STOP.

3. Once cooking is complete, natural release pressure 10 minutes. Release remaining pressure. If desired, press BROWN/SAUTÉ on Express Crock; cook and stir on HIGH 5 minutes or until desired thickness is reached.

SLOW

3 pounds ground beef

2 cans (about 14 ounces *each*) diced tomatoes

2 cans (about 15 ounces *each*) kidney beans, rinsed and drained

2 cups chopped onions

1 package (10 ounces) frozen corn

1 cup chopped green bell pepper

1 can (8 ounces) tomato sauce

3 tablespoons chili powder

1 teaspoon garlic powder

1/2 teaspoon ground cumin

1/2 teaspoon dried oregano

1. Press BROWN/SAUTÉ on **CROCK-POT®** Express Crock Multi-Cooker. Add beef; cook on HIGH 6 to 8 minutes, stirring to break up meat. Drain fat.

2. Add tomatoes, beans, onions, corn, bell pepper, tomato sauce, chili powder, garlic powder, cumin and oregano to Express Crock. Secure lid. Press SLOW COOK, set temperature to LOW and time to 4 hours. Make sure Steam Release Valve is in the "Release" (open) position. Press START/STOP.

3. Once cooking is complete, press BROWN/SAUTÉ on Express Crock, if desired. Cook and stir on HIGH 5 minutes or until desired thickness is reached.

Shredded Chicken Tacos
(*page 132*)

PLEASING POULTRY

BISTRO CHICKEN IN RICH CREAM SAUCE

MAKES 4 SERVINGS

FAST

- **4** skinless, bone-in chicken breasts, rinsed and patted dry (about 3 pounds *total*)
- **½** cup dry white wine
- **1** tablespoon *or* ½ package (1¼ ounces) Italian salad dressing and seasoning mix
- **½** teaspoon dried oregano
- **1** can (10¾ ounces) condensed cream of chicken soup, undiluted
- **3** ounces cream cheese, cubed
- **¼** teaspoon salt
- **⅛** teaspoon black pepper
- **2** tablespoons chopped fresh Italian parsley (optional)

1. Coat inside of **CROCK-POT®** Express Crock Multi-Cooker with nonstick cooking spray. Arrange chicken in single layer in bottom, overlapping slightly. Pour wine over chicken. Sprinkle evenly with salad dressing mix and oregano.

2. Secure lid. Press POULTRY, set pressure to HIGH and time to 15 minutes. Make sure Steam Release Valve is in the "Seal" (closed) position. Press START/STOP.

3. Once cooking is complete, quick release pressure. Remove chicken to large plate using slotted spoon. Press BROWN/SAUTÉ on Express Crock. Whisk soup, cream cheese, salt and pepper into cooking liquid; cook on HIGH 3 minutes or until smooth. To serve, spoon sauce over chicken and garnish with parsley.

SLOW

- **4** skinless, bone-in chicken breasts, rinsed and patted dry (about 3 pounds *total*)
- **½** cup dry white wine
- **1** tablespoon *or* ½ package (1¼ ounces) Italian salad dressing and seasoning mix
- **½** teaspoon dried oregano
- **1** can (10¾ ounces) condensed cream of chicken soup, undiluted
- **3** ounces cream cheese, cubed
- **¼** teaspoon salt
- **⅛** teaspoon black pepper
- **2** tablespoons chopped fresh Italian parsley (optional)

1. Coat inside of **CROCK-POT®** Express Crock Multi-Cooker with nonstick cooking spray. Arrange chicken in single layer in bottom, overlapping slightly. Pour wine over chicken. Sprinkle evenly with salad dressing mix and oregano.

2. Secure lid. Press SLOW COOK, set temperature and time to LOW 5 to 6 hours or to HIGH 2 to 3 hours. Make sure Steam Release Valve is in the "Release" (open) position. Press START/STOP.

3. Once cooking is complete, remove chicken to large plate using slotted spoon. Press BROWN/SAUTÉ on Express Crock. Whisk soup, cream cheese, salt and pepper into cooking liquid; cook on HIGH 3 minutes or until smooth. To serve, spoon sauce over chicken and garnish with parsley.

HAM AND SAGE STUFFED CORNISH HENS

MAKES 4 SERVINGS

FAST

4 tablespoons (½ stick) butter, divided

1 cup plus 3 tablespoons sliced celery, divided

¼ cup finely diced onion

¼ cup diced smoked ham

2 cups seasoned stuffing mix

2 cups chicken broth, divided

1 tablespoon finely chopped fresh sage

4 Cornish hens (about 1½ pounds *each*)

Salt and black pepper

1 cup sliced leek (white part only)

1. Press BROWN/SAUTÉ on **CROCK-POT®** Express Crock Multi-Cooker; heat 1 tablespoon butter on HIGH. Add 3 tablespoons celery, onion and ham; cook and stir 5 minutes or until onion is soft. Stir in stuffing mix, 1 cup broth and sage. Remove mixture to medium bowl. Let stand 10 minutes. Wipe Express Crock clean.

2. Rinse hens and pat dry. Sprinkle inside and outside of each hen with salt and pepper. Gently spoon stuffing evenly into cavities. Tie each hen's drumsticks together with kitchen string. Melt 1 tablespoon butter in Express Crock. Add 2 hens, breast sides down; cook and turn 6 to 8 minutes or until brown. Remove to large plate. Repeat with remaining hens.

3. Place each hen, neck side down, in Express Crock. Add remaining 1 cup celery, leek and remaining 1 cup broth. Secure lid. Press POULTRY, set pressure to HIGH and time to 45 minutes. Make sure Steam Release Valve is in the "Seal" (closed) position. Press START/STOP.

4. Once cooking is complete, natural release pressure 5 minutes. Place hens on large serving platter. Remove and discard string. Press BROWN/SAUTÉ on Express Crock; heat cooking liquid on HIGH 10 minutes. Strain solids; stir in remaining 2 tablespoons butter. Serve hens with gravy.

SLOW

4 tablespoons (½ stick) butter, divided

1 cup plus 3 tablespoons sliced celery, divided

¼ cup finely diced onion

¼ cup diced smoked ham

2 cups seasoned stuffing mix

2 cups chicken broth, divided

1 tablespoon finely chopped fresh sage

4 Cornish hens (about 1½ pounds *each*)

Salt and black pepper

1 cup sliced leek (white part only)

1. Press BROWN/SAUTÉ on **CROCK-POT®** Express Crock Multi-Cooker; heat 1 tablespoon butter on HIGH. Add 3 tablespoons celery, onion and ham; cook and stir 5 minutes or until onion is soft. Stir in stuffing mix, 1 cup broth and sage. Remove mixture to medium bowl. Let stand 10 minutes. Wipe Express Crock clean.

2. Rinse hens and pat dry. Sprinkle inside and outside of each hen with salt and pepper. Gently spoon stuffing evenly into cavities. Tie each hen's drumsticks together with kitchen string. Melt 1 tablespoon butter in Express Crock. Add 2 hens, breast sides down; cook and turn 6 to 8 until browned. Remove to large plate. Repeat with remaining hens.

3. Place each hen, neck side down, in Express Crock. Add remaining 1 cup celery, leek and remaining 1 cup broth. Secure lid. Press SLOW COOK, set temperature and time to LOW 5 to 6 hours or to HIGH 3 to 4 hours. Make sure Steam Release Valve is in the "Release" (open) position. Press START/STOP.

4. Once cooking is complete, natural release pressure 5 minutes. Place hens on large serving platter. Remove and discard string. Press BROWN/SAUTÉ on Express Crock; heat cooking liquid on HIGH 10 minutes. Strain solids; stir in remaining 2 tablespoons butter. Serve hens with gravy.

CARIBBEAN JERK CHICKEN

MAKES 6 SERVINGS

6 boneless, skinless chicken thighs

1 small yellow onion

¼ cup chicken broth

¼ cup soy sauce

1 large jalapeño pepper, seeded*

2 teaspoons minced garlic

1 teaspoon ground ginger

1 teaspoon dried thyme

¼ teaspoon ground cloves

⅛ teaspoon ground allspice

⅛ teaspoon ground cinnamon

Jalapeño pepper slices (optional)*

Hot cooked rice (optional)

Jalapeño peppers can sting and irritate the skin, so wear rubber gloves when handling peppers and do not touch your eyes.

1. Coat inside of **CROCK-POT®** Express Crock Multi-Cooker with nonstick cooking spray; add chicken.

2. Combine onion, broth, soy sauce, jalapeño pepper, garlic, ginger, thyme, cloves, allspice and cinnamon in food processor or blender; process until well blended. Pour onion mixture over chicken in Express Crock. Secure lid. Press POULTRY, set pressure to HIGH and time to 15 minutes. Make sure Steam Release Valve is in the "Seal" (closed) position. Press START/STOP.

3. Once cooking is complete, natural release pressure 10 minutes. Release remaining pressure. Remove chicken to large plate.

4. Press BROWN/SAUTÉ on Express Crock. Cook sauce, uncovered, on HIGH 5 minutes or until thickened. Serve chicken with sauce and rice, if desired.

6 boneless, skinless chicken thighs

1 small yellow onion

¼ cup chicken broth

¼ cup soy sauce

1 large jalapeño pepper, seeded*

2 teaspoons minced garlic

1 teaspoon ground ginger

1 teaspoon dried thyme

¼ teaspoon ground cloves

⅛ teaspoon ground allspice

⅛ teaspoon ground cinnamon

Jalapeño pepper slices (optional)*

Hot cooked rice (optional)

Jalapeño peppers can sting and irritate the skin, so wear rubber gloves when handling peppers and do not touch your eyes.

1. Coat inside of **CROCK-POT®** Express Crock Multi-Cooker with nonstick cooking spray; add chicken.

2. Combine onion, broth, soy sauce, jalapeño pepper, garlic, ginger, thyme, cloves, allspice and cinnamon in food processor or blender; process until well blended. Pour onion mixture over chicken in Express Crock. Secure lid. Press SLOW COOK, set temperature to HIGH and time to 3 hours. Make sure Steam Release Valve is in the "Release" (open) position. Press START/STOP.

3. Once cooking is complete, remove chicken to large plate.

4. Press BROWN/SAUTÉ on Express Crock. Cook sauce, uncovered, on HIGH 10 to 15 minutes or until thickened. Serve chicken with sauce and rice, if desired.

CHILI TURKEY LOAF

MAKES 8 SERVINGS

FAST

1 cup water

2 pounds ground turkey

1 cup chopped onion

²/₃ cup Italian-style seasoned dry bread crumbs

½ cup chopped green bell pepper

½ cup chili sauce

2 eggs, lightly beaten

2 tablespoons horseradish mustard

4 cloves garlic, minced

1 teaspoon salt

½ teaspoon Italian seasoning

¼ teaspoon black pepper

Salsa (optional)

1. Place rack and water in **CROCK-POT®** Express Crock Multi-Cooker. Combine turkey, onion, bread crumbs, bell pepper, chili sauce, eggs, mustard, garlic, salt, Italian seasoning and black pepper in large bowl; mix well. Shape mixture into 7×5-inch oval. Prepare foil handles (page 13).

2. Tear off 18×12-inch piece of foil; fold in half crosswise to create 12×9-inch rectangle. Place meat loaf on foil; bring up sides of foil to create pan, leaving top of meat loaf uncovered. Place foil with meat loaf on rack using foil handles. Secure lid. Press POULTRY, set pressure to HIGH and time to 40 minutes. Make sure Steam Release Valve is in the "Seal" (closed) position. Press START/STOP.

3. Once cooking is complete, quick release pressure. Remove meat loaf to large cutting board, using foil handles. Let stand 5 minutes before serving. Cut into wedges and top with salsa, if desired.

SLOW

1 cup water

2 pounds ground turkey

1 cup chopped onion

²/₃ cup Italian-style seasoned dry bread crumbs

½ cup chopped green bell pepper

½ cup chili sauce

2 eggs, lightly beaten

2 tablespoons horseradish mustard

4 cloves garlic, minced

1 teaspoon salt

½ teaspoon Italian seasoning

¼ teaspoon black pepper

Salsa (optional)

1. Place rack and water in **CROCK-POT®** Express Crock Multi-Cooker. Combine turkey, onion, bread crumbs, bell pepper, chili sauce, eggs, mustard, garlic, salt, Italian seasoning and black pepper in large bowl; mix well. Shape mixture into 7×5-inch oval. Prepare foil handles (page 13).

2. Tear off 18×12-inch piece of foil; fold in half crosswise to create 12×9-inch rectangle. Place meat loaf on foil; bring up sides of foil to create pan, leaving top of meat loaf uncovered. Place foil with meat loaf on rack using foil handles. Secure lid. Press SLOW COOK, set temperature to LOW and time to 5 to 6 hours. Make sure Steam Release Valve is in the "Release" (open) position. Press START/STOP.

3. Once cooking is complete, remove meat loaf to large cutting board using foil handles. Let stand 5 minutes. Cut into wedges and top with salsa, if desired.

CHICKEN CACCIATORE

MAKES 4 SERVINGS

FAST

3 tablespoons olive oil, divided

4 boneless, skinless chicken breasts (about 4 pounds)

Salt and black pepper

1 medium onion, chopped

1 medium green bell pepper, chopped

1 package (8 ounces) sliced button mushrooms

1 teaspoon garlic powder

1 teaspoon dried rosemary

½ teaspoon dried thyme

½ teaspoon red pepper flakes

½ cup chicken broth

2 cans (about 14 ounces each) diced tomatoes with basil and oregano

1 can (6 ounces) tomato paste

Shredded mozzarella cheese (optional)

Hot cooked fettuccine noodles and crusty bread (optional)

1. Press BROWN/SAUTÉ on **CROCK-POT®** Express Crock Multi-Cooker; heat 1 tablespoon oil on HIGH. Season chicken with salt and black pepper. Add chicken to Express Crock; cook chicken in batches 5 to 7 minutes or until browned. Repeat with 1 tablespoon oil and chicken. Remove to large plate.

2. Heat remaining 1 tablespoon oil in Express Crock. Add onion, bell pepper, mushrooms, garlic powder, rosemary, thyme and red pepper flakes; cook and stir 5 minutes until onion is softened. Add chicken and broth. Secure lid. Press POULTRY, set pressure to LOW and time to 15 minutes. Make sure Steam Release Valve is in the "Seal" (closed) position. Press START/STOP.

3. Once cooking is complete, quick release pressure. Remove chicken to large plate. Press BROWN/SAUTÉ on Express Crock. Stir in diced tomatoes and tomato paste; cook on HIGH 5 to 7 minutes or until thickened. Top each serving with cheese, if desired. Serve over noodles with bread, if desired.

SLOW

3 tablespoons olive oil, divided

4 boneless, skinless chicken breasts (about 4 pounds)

Salt and black pepper

1 medium onion, chopped

1 medium green bell pepper, chopped

1 package (8 ounces) sliced button mushrooms

1 teaspoon garlic powder

1 teaspoon dried rosemary

½ teaspoon dried thyme

½ teaspoon red pepper flakes

2 cans (about 14 ounces each) diced tomatoes with basil and oregano

1 can (6 ounces) tomato paste

Shredded mozzarella cheese (optional)

Hot cooked fettuccine noodles and/or crusty bread (optional)

1. Press BROWN/SAUTÉ on **CROCK-POT®** Express Crock Multi-Cooker; heat 1 tablespoon oil on HIGH. Season chicken with salt and black pepper. Add chicken to Express Crock; cook chicken in batches 5 to 7 minutes or until browned. Repeat with 1 tablespoon oil and chicken. Remove to large plate.

2. Heat remaining 1 tablespoon oil in Express Crock. Add onion, bell pepper, mushrooms, garlic powder, rosemary, thyme and red pepper flakes; cook and stir 5 minutes until onion is softened. Stir in diced tomatoes and tomato paste. Add chicken. Secure lid. Press SLOW COOK, set temperature to LOW and time to 6 hours. Make sure Steam Release Valve is in the "Release" (open) position. Press START/STOP.

3. Once cooking is complete, top each serving with cheese, if desired. Serve over noodles with bread, if desired.

CHICKEN SALTIMBOCCA-STYLE

MAKES 6 SERVINGS

FAST

6 boneless, skinless chicken breasts	1/2 cup grated Parmesan cheese	2 cans (10 3/4 ounces *each*) condensed cream of mushroom soup, undiluted
12 slices prosciutto	2 teaspoons salt	
12 slices provolone cheese	2 teaspoons black pepper	3/4 cup dry white wine
1/2 cup all-purpose flour	Olive oil	1 teaspoon ground sage

1. Split each chicken breast into two thin pieces. Place between two pieces of waxed paper or plastic wrap; pound until 1/3 inch thick. Place 1 slice of prosciutto and 1 slice of provolone on each chicken piece and roll up. Secure with toothpicks.

2. Combine flour, Parmesan cheese, salt and pepper on large rimmed plate. Dredge chicken in flour mixture, shaking off excess. Reserve excess flour mixture. Heat oil in **CROCK-POT®** Express Crock Multi-Cooker. Add chicken in batches; cook 5 to 7 minutes or until browned on both sides. Remove to large plate.

3. Add chicken, soup, wine and sage to Express Crock. Secure lid. Press POULTRY, set pressure to LOW and time to 15 minutes. Make sure Steam Release Valve is in the "Seal" (closed) position. Press START/STOP.

4. Once cooking is complete, quick release pressure. Remove chicken to large serving platter. Press BROWN/SAUTÉ on Express Crock. Add 2 tablespoons cooking liquid to reserved flour mixture; whisk until smooth. Whisk flour mixture into Express Crock; cook on HIGH 15 minutes or until thickened. Serve chicken with sauce.

SLOW

6 boneless, skinless chicken breasts	1/2 cup grated Parmesan cheese	2 cans (10 3/4 ounces *each*) condensed cream of mushroom soup, undiluted
12 slices prosciutto	2 teaspoons salt	
12 slices provolone cheese	2 teaspoons black pepper	3/4 cup dry white wine
1/2 cup all-purpose flour	Olive oil	1 teaspoon ground sage

1. Split each chicken breast into two thin pieces. Place between two pieces of waxed paper or plastic wrap; pound until 1/3 inch thick. Place 1 slice of prosciutto and 1 slice of provolone on each chicken piece and roll up. Secure with toothpicks.

2. Combine flour, Parmesan cheese, salt and pepper on large rimmed plate. Dredge chicken in flour mixture, shaking off excess. Reserve excess flour mixture. Heat oil in **CROCK-POT®** Express Crock Multi-Cooker. Add chicken in batches; cook 5 to 7 minutes or until browned on both sides. Remove to large plate.

3. Add chicken, soup, wine and sage to Express Crock. Secure lid. Press SLOW COOK, set temperature and time to LOW 5 to 7 hours or to HIGH 2 to 3 hours. Make sure Steam Release Valve is in the "Release" (open) position. Press START/STOP.

4. Once cooking is complete, remove chicken to large serving platter. Press BROWN/SAUTÉ on Express Crock. Add 2 tablespoons cooking liquid to reserved flour mixture; whisk until smooth. Whisk flour mixture into Express Crock; cook on HIGH 15 minutes or until thickened. Serve chicken with sauce.

DENVER EGG BOWLS

MAKES 4 SERVINGS

FAST

1¾ cups water, divided
4 bell peppers, any color
8 eggs

3 green onions, chopped
¼ cup diced ham

1 cup (4 ounces) shredded Cheddar cheese
Paprika

1. Add 1 cup water to 6- to 7-inch (1½-quart) soufflé dish or round baking dish that fits inside of **CROCK-POT®** Express Crock Multi-Cooker. Prepare foil handles (page 13). Place rack in Express Crock; add remaining ¾ cup water.

2. Cut thin slice off top of each bell pepper; reserve tops. Carefully remove and discard seeds and membranes, leaving peppers whole. Dice bell pepper tops; measure ¼ cup. Discard remaining diced bell pepper or reserve for another use.

3. Whisk eggs, ¼ cup diced bell peppers and green onions in large measuring cup until well blended. Pour egg mixture evenly into each pepper; top each pepper with ham. Place peppers in bottom of prepared dish. Place dish on rack using foil handles. Secure lid. Press STEAM, set pressure to HIGH and time to 7 minutes. Make sure Steam Release Valve is in the "Seal" (closed) position. Press START/STOP.

4. Once cooking is complete, quick release pressure. Sprinkle with cheese and paprika.

SLOW

1¾ cups water, divided
4 bell peppers, any color
8 eggs

3 green onions, chopped
¼ cup diced ham

1 cup (4 ounces) shredded Cheddar cheese
Paprika

1. Add 1 cup water to 6- to 7-inch (1½-quart) soufflé dish or round baking dish that fits inside of **CROCK-POT®** Express Crock Multi-Cooker. Prepare foil handles (page 13). Place rack in Express Crock; add remaining ¾ cup water.

2. Cut thin slice off top of each bell pepper; reserve tops. Carefully remove and discard seeds and membranes, leaving peppers whole. Dice pepper tops; measure ¼ cup. Discard remaining diced pepper or reserve for another use.

3. Whisk eggs, ¼ cup diced peppers and green onions in large measuring cup until well blended. Pour egg mixture evenly into each pepper; top each pepper with ham. Place peppers in bottom of prepared dish. Place dish on rack using foil handles. Secure lid. Press SLOW COOK, set temperature to HIGH and time to 3½ hours. Make sure Steam Release Valve is in the "Release" (open) position. Press START/STOP.

4. Once cooking is complete, sprinkle with cheese and paprika.

TERIYAKI CHICKEN

MAKES 4 SERVINGS

FAST

1 can (6 ounces) pineapple juice

¼ cup soy sauce

1 tablespoon sugar

1 tablespoon minced fresh ginger

1 tablespoon minced garlic

1 tablespoon vegetable oil

1 tablespoon molasses

1 pound boneless, skinless chicken tenders

24 cherry tomatoes

2 cups hot cooked rice

Chopped fresh chives (optional)

1. Combine pineapple juice, soy sauce, sugar, ginger, garlic, oil and molasses in **CROCK-POT®** Express Crock Multi-Cooker; stir to dissolve sugar. Add chicken and tomatoes; stir to coat. Secure lid. Press POULTRY, set pressure to HIGH and time to 15 minutes. Make sure Steam Release Valve is in the "Seal" (closed) position. Press START/STOP.

2. Once cooking is complete, natural release pressure 10 minutes. Release remaining pressure. Serve chicken and sauce over rice. Garnish with chives.

SLOW

1 can (6 ounces) pineapple juice

¼ cup soy sauce

1 tablespoon sugar

1 tablespoon minced fresh ginger

1 tablespoon minced garlic

1 tablespoon vegetable oil

1 tablespoon molasses

1 pound boneless, skinless chicken tenders

24 cherry tomatoes

2 cups hot cooked rice

Chopped fresh chives (optional)

1. Combine pineapple juice, soy sauce, sugar, ginger, garlic, oil and molasses in **CROCK-POT®** Express Crock Multi-Cooker; stir to dissolve sugar. Add chicken and tomatoes; stir to coat. Secure lid. Press SLOW COOK, set temperature to LOW and time to 2 hours. Make sure Steam Release Valve is in the "Release" (open) position. Press START/STOP.

2. Once cooking is complete, serve chicken and sauce over rice. Garnish with chives.

VEGETABLE EGG NESTS

MAKES 4 SERVINGS

FAST

1 **cup water**

1 **package (12 ounces) frozen butternut squash spirals, thawed**

1 **teaspoon vegetable oil**

¼ **teaspoon salt, plus additional for serving**

¼ **teaspoon ground nutmeg**

¼ **teaspoon black pepper, plus additional for serving**

4 **eggs**

1. Line four 6- to 8-ounce ramekins with square of parchment paper; spray parchment with nonstick cooking spray. Place rack in **CROCK-POT®** Express Crock Multi-Cooker; add water.

2. Combine butternut squash spirals, oil, ¼ teaspoon salt, nutmeg and ¼ teaspoon pepper in medium bowl; toss to coat. Arrange butternut squash spirals evenly in prepared ramekins. Crack one egg over squash in each ramekin. Add ramekins to Express Crock. Secure lid. Press STEAM, set pressure to HIGH and time to 5 minutes. Make sure Steam Release Valve is in the "Seal" (closed) position. Press START/STOP.

3. Once cooking is complete, quick release pressure. Remove nests from ramekins using parchment to plates, if desired. Season with additional salt and black pepper.

SLOW

1 **cup water**

1 **package (12 ounces) frozen butternut squash spirals, thawed**

1 **teaspoon vegetable oil**

¼ **teaspoon salt, plus additional for serving**

¼ **teaspoon ground nutmeg**

¼ **teaspoon black pepper, plus additional for serving**

4 **eggs**

1. Line four 6- to 8-ounce ramekins with square of parchment paper; spray parchment with nonstick cooking spray. Place rack in **CROCK-POT®** Express Crock Multi-Cooker; add water.

2. Combine butternut squash spirals, oil, ¼ teaspoon salt, nutmeg and ¼ teaspoon pepper in medium bowl; toss to coat. Arrange butternut squash spirals evenly in prepared ramekins. Crack one egg over squash in each ramekin. Add ramekins to Express Crock. Secure lid. Press SLOW COOK, set temperature to HIGH and time to 2 hours or to desired egg doneness. Make sure Steam Release Valve is in the "Release" (open) position. Press START/STOP.

3. Once cooking is complete, remove nests from ramekins using parchment to plates, if desired. Season with additional salt and black pepper.

CHICKEN RAMEN NOODLE BOWLS

MAKES 6 SERVINGS

FAST

1 tablespoon olive oil

1 pound boneless, skinless chicken thighs

1 large yellow onion, peeled and halved

6 cups chicken broth

2 tablespoons soy sauce

4 green onions, divided

1 (1-inch) piece fresh ginger, sliced

1 clove garlic

6 ounces shiitake mushrooms, thinly sliced

1/3 cup hoisin sauce

8 ounces uncooked fresh Chinese noodles

3 hard-cooked eggs, cut in half lengthwise

1/4 cup thinly sliced red bell pepper

Fresh cilantro leaves

1. Press BROWN/SAUTÉ on **CROCK-POT®** Express Crock Multi-Cooker; heat oil on HIGH. Add chicken in batches; cook 5 to 7 minutes or until browned. Remove to large plate.

2. Add onion halves to Express Crock, cut side down; cook 4 to 5 minutes or until lightly charred. Add broth, chicken, soy sauce, 2 green onions, ginger and garlic to Express Crock. Secure lid. Press SOUP, set pressure to HIGH and time to 15 minutes. Make sure Steam Release Valve is in the "Seal" (closed) position. Press START/STOP.

3. Once cooking is complete, quick release pressure. Remove chicken to large cutting board; shred with two forks. Strain broth into large bowl. Discard solids; return broth to Express Crock. Stir in mushrooms and hoisin sauce. Divide noodles and broth evenly among six bowls. Top each bowl evenly with chicken, mushrooms, one egg half, bell pepper and cilantro. Chop remaining 2 green onions; sprinkle evenly over bowls.

SLOW

1 tablespoon olive oil

1 pound boneless, skinless chicken thighs

1 large yellow onion, peeled and halved

6 cups chicken broth

2 tablespoons soy sauce

4 green onions, divided

1 (1-inch) piece fresh ginger, sliced

1 clove garlic

6 ounces shiitake mushrooms, thinly sliced

1/3 cup hoisin sauce

8 ounces uncooked fresh Chinese noodles

3 hard-cooked eggs, cut in half lengthwise

1/4 cup thinly sliced red bell pepper

Fresh cilantro leaves

1. Press BROWN/SAUTÉ on **CROCK-POT®** Express Crock Multi-Cooker; heat oil on HIGH. Add chicken; cook 5 to 7 minutes or until browned on both sides. Remove to large plate.

2. Add onion halves to Express Crock, cut side down; cook 4 to 5 minutes or until lightly charred. Add broth, chicken, soy sauce, 2 green onions, ginger and garlic to Express Crock. Secure lid. Press SLOW COOK, set temperature and time to LOW 6 to 7 hours or to HIGH 3 to 4 hours. Make sure Steam Release Valve is in the "Release" (open) position. Press START/STOP.

3. Once cooking is complete, remove chicken to large cutting board; shred with two forks. Strain broth into large bowl. Discard solids; return broth to Express Crock. Stir in mushrooms and hoisin sauce. Divide

noodles and broth evenly among six bowls. Top each bowl evenly with chicken, mushrooms, one egg half, bell pepper and cilantro. Chop remaining 2 green onions; sprinkle evenly over bowls.

CHICKEN PARMESAN WITH EGGPLANT

MAKES 4 SERVINGS

FAST

- 2 boneless, skinless chicken breasts
- 2 eggs
- 1 teaspoon salt
- 1 teaspoon black pepper
- ³/₄ cup seasoned dry bread crumbs
- ¹/₄ cup olive oil
- 1¹/₂ cups water
- 1 small eggplant, cut into ³/₄-inch-thick slices
- ¹/₂ cup grated Parmesan cheese
- 1 cup tomato-basil pasta sauce
- 1 cup (4 ounces) shredded mozzarella cheese
- Sprigs fresh basil (optional)

1. Slice chicken breasts in half lengthwise. Cut each half lengthwise again to get four ¹/₂-inch slices. Combine eggs, salt and pepper in medium bowl; whisk to blend. Place bread crumbs in separate medium bowl. Dip chicken in egg mixture; turn to coat. Dip chicken in bread crumbs; turn to coat.

2. Press BROWN/SAUTÉ on **CROCK-POT®** Express Crock Multi-Cooker; heat oil on HIGH. Add breaded chicken; cook 6 to 8 minutes or until browned on both sides. Remove to paper towel-lined plate. Wipe out Express Crock.

3. Spray 6- to 7-inch (1¹/₂-quart) soufflé dish or round baking dish that fits inside of Express Crock with nonstick cooking spray. Prepare foil handles (page 13). Place rack in Express Crock; add water.

4. Layer half of eggplant, ¹/₄ cup Parmesan cheese and ¹/₂ cup sauce in prepared dish. Top with half of chicken, remaining half of eggplant, remaining ¹/₄ cup Parmesan cheese and ¹/₂ cup sauce. Top with mozzarella cheese. Secure lid. Press MEAT/STEW, set pressure to HIGH and time to 15 minutes. Make sure Steam Release Valve is in the "Seal" (closed) position. Press START/STOP.

5. Once cooking is complete, quick release pressure. Remove dish using foil handles; let stand 5 minutes. Garnish with basil.

SLOW

- 2 boneless, skinless chicken breasts
- 2 eggs
- 1 teaspoon salt
- 1 teaspoon black pepper
- ³/₄ cup seasoned dry bread crumbs
- ¹/₄ cup olive oil
- 1¹/₂ cups water
- 1 small eggplant, cut into ³/₄-inch-thick slices
- ¹/₂ cup grated Parmesan cheese
- 1 cup tomato-basil pasta sauce
- ¹/₂ cup (2 ounces) shredded mozzarella cheese
- Sprigs fresh basil (optional)

1. Slice chicken breasts in half lengthwise. Cut each half lengthwise again to get four ³/₄-inch slices. Combine eggs, salt and pepper in medium bowl; whisk to blend. Place bread crumbs in separate medium bowl. Dip chicken in egg mixture; turn to coat. Then coat chicken with bread crumbs, covering both sides evenly.

2. Press BROWN/SAUTÉ on **CROCK-POT®** Express Crock Multi-Cooker; heat oil on HIGH. Add breaded chicken; cook 6 to 8 minutes until browned on both sides. Remove to paper towel-lined plate to drain excess oil.

3. Spray 6- to 7-inch (1½-quart) soufflé dish or round baking dish that fits inside of Express Crock with nonstick cooking spray. Prepare foil handles (page 13). Place rack in Express Crock; add water.

4. Layer half of eggplant, ¼ cup Parmesan cheese and ½ cup sauce in prepared dish. Top with half of chicken, remaining half of eggplant, remaining ¼ cup Parmesan cheese and ½ cup sauce. Top with mozzarella cheese. Secure lid. Press SLOW COOK, set temperature and time to LOW 4 hours or to HIGH 2 hours. Make sure Steam Release Valve is in the "Release" (open) position. Press START/STOP.

5. Once cooking is complete, remove dish using foil handles. Garnish with basil.

BEER CHICKEN

MAKES 4 TO 6 SERVINGS

FAST

2 tablespoons olive oil	4 medium carrots, chopped into 1-inch pieces	1 teaspoon salt
1 cut-up whole chicken (3 to 5 pounds)	1 cup sliced celery	1/2 teaspoon black pepper
10 new potatoes, halved	1 medium onion, chopped	2 tablespoons water
1 can (12 ounces) beer	1 tablespoon chopped fresh rosemary	2 tablespoons all-purpose flour

1. Press BROWN/SAUTÉ on **CROCK-POT®** Express Crock Multi-Cooker; heat oil on HIGH. Add chicken in batches; cook, uncovered, 5 to 7 minutes or until browned. Remove to large paper towel-lined plate.

2. Add chicken, potatoes, beer, carrots, celery, onion, rosemary, salt and pepper to Express Crock. Secure lid. Press POULTRY, set pressure to HIGH and time to 15 minutes. Make sure Steam Release Valve is in the "Seal" (closed) position. Press START/STOP.

3. Once cooking is complete, quick release pressure. Remove chicken and potato mixture to large serving platter using slotted spoon; keep warm. Press BROWN/SAUTÉ on Express Crock. Stir water into flour in small bowl until smooth; whisk into cooking liquid. Cook, uncovered, on HIGH 10 to 15 minutes or until thickened. Serve chicken and vegetables with sauce.

SLOW

2 tablespoons olive oil	4 medium carrots, chopped into 1-inch pieces	1 teaspoon salt
1 cut-up whole chicken (3 to 5 pounds)	1 cup sliced celery	1/2 teaspoon black pepper
10 new potatoes, halved	1 medium onion, chopped	2 tablespoons water
1 can (12 ounces) beer	1 tablespoon chopped fresh rosemary	2 tablespoons all-purpose flour

1. Press BROWN/SAUTÉ on **CROCK-POT®** Express Crock Multi-Cooker; heat oil on HIGH. Add chicken in batches; cook, uncovered, 5 to 7 minutes or until browned. Remove to large paper towel-lined plate.

2. Add chicken, potatoes, beer, carrots, celery, onion, rosemary, salt and pepper to Express Crock. Secure lid. Press SLOW COOK, set temperature to HIGH and time to 5 hours. Make sure Steam Release Valve is in the "Release" (open) position. Press START/STOP.

3. Once cooking is complete, remove chicken and potato mixture to large bowl using slotted spoon; keep warm. Press BROWN/SAUTÉ on Express Crock. Stir water into flour in small bowl until smooth; whisk into cooking liquid. Cook, uncovered, on HIGH 10 to 15 minutes or until thickened. Serve chicken and vegetables with sauce.

ASIAN LETTUCE WRAPS

MAKES 6 SERVINGS

FAST

2 teaspoons canola oil

1½ pounds boneless, skinless chicken breasts, chopped into ¼-inch pieces

2 leeks, trimmed and chopped into ¼-inch pieces

1 cup shiitake mushrooms, stems removed and caps chopped into ¼-inch pieces

1 stalk celery, chopped into ¼-inch pieces

1 tablespoon oyster sauce

1 tablespoon soy sauce

1 teaspoon dark sesame oil

¼ teaspoon black pepper

½ pound large raw shrimp, peeled, deveined and cut into ¼-inch pieces

1 bag (8 ounces) coleslaw or broccoli slaw mix

½ red bell pepper, cut into thin strips

3 tablespoons unsalted dry roasted peanuts, coarsely chopped

Hoisin sauce

12 crisp romaine lettuce leaves, white ribs removed and patted dry

Fresh whole chives

1. Press BROWN/SAUTÉ on **CROCK-POT®** Express Crock Multi-Cooker; heat canola oil on HIGH. Add chicken; cook, uncovered, 5 minutes or until browned on all sides. Add leeks, mushrooms, celery, oyster sauce, soy sauce, sesame oil and black pepper; stir to blend. Secure lid. Press BEANS/CHILI, set pressure to HIGH and time to 5 minutes. Make sure Steam Release Valve is in the "Seal" (closed) position. Press START/STOP.

2. Once cooking is complete, natural release pressure 10 minutes. Release remaining pressure. Press BROWN/SAUTÉ on Express Crock. Stir in shrimp, slaw mix and bell pepper; cook, uncovered, on HIGH 3 to 5 minutes or until shrimp are pink and opaque. Remove mixture to large bowl; stir in peanuts.

3. To serve, spread hoisin sauce on lettuce leaves. Add meat mixture and tightly roll; secure by tying chives around rolled leaves.

SLOW

2 teaspoons canola oil

1½ pounds boneless, skinless chicken breasts, chopped into ¼-inch pieces

2 leeks, trimmed and chopped into ¼-inch pieces

1 cup shiitake mushrooms, stems removed and caps chopped into ¼-inch pieces

1 stalk celery, chopped into ¼-inch pieces

1 tablespoon oyster sauce

1 tablespoon soy sauce

1 teaspoon dark sesame oil

¼ teaspoon black pepper

2 tablespoons water

1 bag (8 ounces) coleslaw or broccoli slaw mix

½ red bell pepper, cut into thin strips

½ pound large raw shrimp, peeled, deveined and cut into ¼-inch pieces

3 tablespoons dry roasted peanuts, coarsely chopped

Hoisin sauce

12 crisp romaine lettuce leaves, white ribs removed and patted dry

Fresh whole chives

1. Press BROWN/SAUTÉ on **CROCK-POT®** Express Crock Multi-Cooker; heat canola oil on HIGH. Add chicken; cook, uncovered, 5 minutes or until browned on all sides. Add leeks, mushrooms, celery, oyster sauce, soy sauce, sesame oil, black pepper and water to Express Crock. Toss slaw and bell pepper in medium bowl; place in single layer on top of chicken mixture.

2. Secure lid. Press SLOW COOK, set temperature and time to LOW 4 to 5 hours or to HIGH 2 to 2$\frac{1}{2}$ hours. Make sure Steam Release Valve is in the "Release" (open) position. Press START/STOP. Stir in shrimp during last 20 minutes of cooking.

3. Once cooking is complete, chicken is cooked through and shrimp are pink and opaque; stir in peanuts. To serve, spread hoisin sauce on lettuce leaves. Add meat mixture and tightly roll; secure by tying chives around rolled leaves.

MIXED HERB AND BUTTER RUBBED CHICKEN

MAKES 4 TO 6 SERVINGS

3 tablespoons butter, softened

1 tablespoon grated lemon peel

2 teaspoons fresh rosemary

1 teaspoon chopped fresh thyme

³/₄ teaspoon salt

¹/₄ teaspoon black pepper

1 whole chicken (4¹/₂ to 5 pounds)

1 cup chicken broth

2 tablespoons water

2 tablespoons all-purpose flour

1. Coat inside of **CROCK-POT®** Express Crock Multi-Cooker with nonstick cooking spray. Combine butter, lemon peel, rosemary, thyme, salt and pepper in small bowl; stir to blend. Loosen skin over breast meat and drumsticks; pat chicken dry with paper towels. Rub butter mixture over and under chicken skin.

2. Pour broth into Express Crock; add chicken. Secure lid. Press POULTRY, set pressure to HIGH and time to 45 minutes. Make sure Steam Release Valve is in the "Seal" (closed) position. Press START/STOP.

3. Once cooking is complete, natural release pressure 5 minutes. Release remaining pressure. Remove chicken to large cutting board. Cover loosely with foil; let stand 10 minutes before cutting into pieces.

4. Meanwhile, press BROWN/SAUTÉ on Express Crock. Bring cooking liquid to a boil on HIGH. Stir water into flour in small bowl until smooth; whisk into cooking liquid. Cook, uncovered, on HIGH 10 to 15 minutes or until thickened. Serve chicken with gravy.

3 tablespoons butter, softened

1 tablespoon grated lemon peel

2 teaspoons chopped fresh rosemary

1 teaspoon chopped fresh thyme

³/₄ teaspoon salt

¹/₄ teaspoon black pepper

1 whole chicken (4¹/₂ to 5 pounds)

1 cup chicken broth

2 tablespoons water

2 tablespoons all-purpose flour

1. Coat inside of **CROCK-POT®** Express Crock Multi-Cooker with nonstick cooking spray. Combine butter, lemon peel, rosemary, thyme, salt and pepper in small bowl; stir to blend. Loosen skin over breast meat and drumsticks; pat chicken dry with paper towels. Rub butter mixture over and under chicken skin.

2. Pour broth into Express Crock; add chicken. Secure lid. Press SLOW COOK, set temperature to LOW and time to 5 to 6 hours, basting every 30 minutes with cooking liquid. Make sure Steam Release Valve is in the "Release" (open) position. Press START/STOP.

3. Once cooking is complete, remove chicken to large cutting board. Cover loosely with foil; let stand 10 minutes before cutting into pieces.

4. Meanwhile, press BROWN/SAUTÉ on Express Crock. Bring cooking liquid to a boil on HIGH. Stir water into flour in small bowl until smooth; whisk into cooking liquid. Cook, uncovered, on HIGH 10 to 15 minutes or until thickened. Serve chicken with gravy.

CHIPOTLE TURKEY SLOPPY JOE SLIDERS

MAKES 12 SLIDERS

FAST

1 **pound turkey Italian sausage links, casings removed**

1 **package (14 ounces) frozen green and red bell pepper strips with onions**

1 **cup chicken broth**

1 **can (6 ounces) tomato paste**

1 **tablespoon quick-cooking tapioca**

1 **tablespoon minced canned chipotle peppers in adobo sauce, plus 1 tablespoon sauce**

2 **teaspoons ground cumin**

1/2 **teaspoon dried thyme**

12 **corn muffins or small dinner rolls, split and toasted**

1. Press BROWN/SAUTÉ on **CROCK-POT®** Express Crock Multi-Cooker. Add sausage; cook, uncovered, on HIGH 6 to 8 minutes, stirring to break up meat. Drain fat. Add pepper strips with onions, broth, tomato paste, tapioca, chipotle peppers with sauce, cumin and thyme; stir to blend. Secure lid. Press POULTRY, set pressure to HIGH and time to 15 minutes. Make sure Steam Release Valve is in the "Seal" (closed) position. Press START/STOP.

2. Once cooking is complete, quick release pressure. Serve on corn muffins.

SLOW

1 **pound turkey Italian sausage links, casings removed**

1 **package (14 ounces) frozen green and red bell pepper strips with onions**

1 **can (6 ounces) tomato paste**

1 **tablespoon quick-cooking tapioca**

1 **tablespoon minced canned chipotle peppers in adobo sauce, plus 1 tablespoon sauce**

2 **teaspoons ground cumin**

1/2 **teaspoon dried thyme**

12 **corn muffins or small dinner rolls, split and toasted**

1. Press BROWN/SAUTÉ on **CROCK-POT®** Express Crock Multi-Cooker. Add sausage; cook, uncovered, on HIGH 6 to 8 minutes or until browned, stirring to break up meat. Drain fat. Stir in pepper strips with onions, tomato paste, tapioca, chipotle peppers with sauce, cumin and thyme. Secure lid. Press SLOW COOK, set temperature to LOW and time to 8 hours. Make sure Steam Release Valve is in the "Release" (open) position. Press START/STOP.

2. Once cooking is complete, serve on corn muffins.

CHICKEN FAJITAS WITH BARBECUE SAUCE

MAKES 4 SERVINGS

FAST

1 tablespoon olive oil

10 ounces boneless, skinless chicken breasts, cut into ½-inch strips

Salt and black pepper

1 can (8 ounces) tomato sauce

⅓ cup chopped green onions

¼ cup ketchup

2 tablespoons water

2 tablespoons orange juice

1 tablespoon cider vinegar

1 tablespoon chili sauce

2 cloves garlic, finely chopped

Dash Worcestershire sauce

2 green or red bell peppers, thinly sliced

1 cup sliced onion

4 (6-inch) flour tortillas, warmed

Tomato wedges

1. Press BROWN/SAUTÉ on **CROCK-POT®** Express Crock Multi-Cooker; heat oil on HIGH. Season chicken with salt and black pepper. Add chicken to Express Crock; cook 5 to 7 minutes or until browned. Remove to large plate.

2. Combine tomato sauce, green onions, ketchup, water, orange juice, vinegar, chili sauce, garlic and Worcestershire sauce in Express Crock; stir to blend. Top with chicken, bell peppers and onion. Secure lid. Press BEANS/CHILI, set pressure to HIGH and time to 7 minutes. Make sure Steam Release Valve is in the "Seal" (closed) position. Press START/STOP.

3. Once cooking is complete, quick release pressure. If desired, removed chicken and vegetables to large bowl. Press BROWN/SAUTÉ on Express Crock; heat cooking liquid, uncovered, on HIGH 5 to 7 minutes or until desired thickness. Serve chicken, vegetables and cooking liquid with tortillas and tomatoes.

SLOW

1 tablespoon olive oil

10 ounces boneless, skinless chicken breasts, cut into ½-inch strips

Salt and black pepper

1 can (8 ounces) tomato sauce

⅓ cup chopped green onions

¼ cup ketchup

2 tablespoons water

2 tablespoons orange juice

1 tablespoon cider vinegar

1 tablespoon chili sauce

2 cloves garlic, finely chopped

Dash Worcestershire sauce

2 green or red bell peppers, thinly sliced

1 cup sliced onion

2 cups tomato wedges

4 (6-inch) flour tortillas, warmed

1. Press BROWN/SAUTÉ on **CROCK-POT®** Express Crock Multi-Cooker; heat oil on HIGH. Season chicken with salt and black pepper. Add chicken to Express Crock; cook 5 to 7 minutes or until browned. Remove to large plate.

2. Combine tomato sauce, green onions, ketchup, water, orange juice, vinegar, chili sauce, garlic and Worcestershire sauce in Express Crock; stir to blend. Top with chicken, bell peppers and onion. Secure lid. Press SLOW COOK, set temperature to LOW and time to 3 to 4 hours. Make sure Steam Release Valve is in the "Release" (open) position. Press START/STOP.

3. Add tomato wedges to Express Crock. Secure lid. Press SLOW COOK, set temperature to LOW and time to 30 to 45 minutes. Make sure Steam Release Valve is in the "Release" (open) position. Press START/STOP.

4. Once cooking is complete, serve chicken, vegetables and sauce with tortillas.

SALSA-STYLE WINGS

MAKES 4 SERVINGS

FAST

2 tablespoons vegetable oil	2 cups salsa, plus additional for serving	Sprigs fresh cilantro (optional)
1½ pounds chicken wings (about 18 wings)	¼ cup packed brown sugar	

1. Press BROWN/SAUTÉ on **CROCK-POT®** Express Crock Multi-Cooker; heat oil on HIGH. Add wings in batches; cook, uncovered, 3 to 4 minutes or until browned on all sides.

2. Combine 2 cups salsa and brown sugar in medium bowl; stir to blend. Pour over wings. Secure lid. Press POULTRY, set pressure to HIGH and time to 15 minutes. Make sure Steam Release Valve is in the "Seal" (closed) position. Press START/STOP.

3. Once cooking is complete, quick release pressure. Remove wings to large bowl. Turn off heat. Let sauce stand 5 minutes. Skim off and discard fat. Press BROWN/SAUTÉ on Express Crock; cook sauce, uncovered, on HIGH 5 minutes or until reduced by half. Pour sauce over wings. Serve with additional salsa; garnish with cilantro.

SLOW

2 tablespoons vegetable oil	2 cups salsa, plus additional for serving	Sprigs fresh cilantro (optional)
1½ pounds chicken wings (about 18 wings)	¼ cup packed brown sugar	

1. Press BROWN/SAUTÉ on **CROCK-POT®** Express Crock Multi-Cooker; heat oil on HIGH. Add wings in batches; cook, uncovered, 3 to 4 minutes or until browned on all sides.

2. Combine 2 cups salsa and brown sugar in medium bowl; stir to blend. Pour over wings. Secure lid. Press SLOW COOK, set temperature and time to LOW 5 to 6 hours or to HIGH 2 to 3 hours. Make sure Steam Release Valve is in the "Release" (open) position. Press START/STOP.

3. Once cooking is complete, remove wings to large bowl. Turn off heat. Let sauce stand 5 minutes. Skim off and discard fat. Press BROWN/SAUTÉ on Express Crock; cook sauce, uncovered, on HIGH 5 minutes or until reduced by half. Pour sauce over wings. Serve with additional salsa; garnish with cilantro.

ANGELIC DEVILED EGGS

MAKES 12 SERVINGS

FAST

1½ cups water
6 eggs
¼ cup cottage cheese

3 tablespoons ranch dressing
2 teaspoons Dijon mustard
2 tablespoons minced fresh dill

1 tablespoon diced well-drained pimientos
Sprigs fresh dill (optional)

1. Place rack in **CROCK-POT®** Express Crock Multi-Cooker; add water. Place eggs on rack. Secure lid. Press STEAM, set pressure to LOW and time to 10 minutes. Make sure Steam Release Valve is in the "Seal" (closed) position. Press START/STOP.

2. Once cooking is complete, quick release pressure. Remove eggs to large bowl of ice water; let cool 5 to 10 minutes.

3. Peel eggs; cut in half lengthwise. Remove yolks, reserving 3 yolk halves. Discard remaining yolks or reserve for another use. Place egg whites, cut sides up, on serving plate; cover with plastic wrap. Refrigerate while preparing filling.

4. Combine cottage cheese, dressing, mustard and reserved yolk halves in small bowl; mash with fork until well blended. Stir in dill and pimientos. Spoon cottage cheese mixture into egg whites. Cover; refrigerate at least 1 hour before serving. Garnish with dill sprigs.

SLOW

1½ cups water
6 eggs
¼ cup cottage cheese

3 tablespoons ranch dressing
2 teaspoons Dijon mustard
2 tablespoons minced fresh dill

1 tablespoon diced well-drained pimientos or roasted red pepper
Sprigs fresh dill (optional)

1. Place rack in **CROCK-POT®** Express Crock Multi-Cooker; add water. Place eggs on rack. Secure lid. Press SLOW COOK, set temperature to LOW and time to 3½ hours. Make sure Steam Release Valve is in the "Release" (open) position. Press START/STOP.

2. Once cooking is complete, remove eggs to large bowl of ice water. Let cool 5 to 10 minutes.

3. Peel eggs; cut eggs in half lengthwise. Remove yolks, reserving 3 yolk halves. Discard remaining yolks or reserve for another use. Place egg whites, cut sides up, on serving plate; cover with plastic wrap. Refrigerate while preparing filling.

4. Combine cottage cheese, dressing, mustard and reserved yolk halves in small bowl; mash with fork until well blended. Stir in dill and pimientos. Spoon cottage cheese mixture into egg whites. Cover; refrigerate at least 1 hour before serving. Garnish with dill sprigs.

SHREDDED CHICKEN TACOS

MAKES 4 SERVINGS

FAST

2 pounds boneless, skinless chicken thighs

³/₄ cup mango salsa, plus additional for serving

Lettuce (optional)

8 (6-inch) yellow corn tortillas, warmed

1. Coat inside of **CROCK-POT®** Express Crock Multi-Cooker with nonstick cooking spray. Add chicken and ¹/₂ cup salsa. Secure lid. Press POULTRY, set pressure to HIGH and time to 15 minutes. Make sure Steam Release Valve is in the "Seal" (closed) position. Press START/STOP.

2. Once cooking is complete, natural release pressure 10 minutes. Release remaining pressure. Remove chicken to large cutting board; shred with two forks. Stir shredded chicken back into Express Crock. To serve, divide chicken and lettuce, if desired, evenly among tortillas. Serve with additional salsa.

SLOW

2 pounds boneless, skinless chicken thighs

¹/₂ cup mango salsa, plus additional for serving

Lettuce (optional)

8 (6-inch) yellow corn tortillas, warmed

1. Coat inside of **CROCK-POT®** Express Crock Multi-Cooker with nonstick cooking spray. Add chicken and ¹/₂ cup salsa. Secure lid. Press SLOW COOK, set temperature and time to LOW 4 to 5 hours or to HIGH 2¹/₂ to 3 hours. Make sure Steam Release Valve is in the "Release" (open) position. Press START/STOP.

2. Once cooking is complete, remove chicken to large cutting board; shred with two forks. Stir shredded chicken back into Express Crock. To serve, divide chicken and lettuce, if desired, evenly among tortillas. Serve with additional salsa.

Italian Meatball Hoagies
(page 154)

BEEF AND PORK

BARBECUE BEEF SLIDERS

MAKES 6 SERVINGS

1 tablespoon packed light brown sugar

1 teaspoon ground cumin

1 teaspoon chili powder

1 teaspoon paprika

½ teaspoon salt

¼ teaspoon ground red pepper

1 boneless beef bottom round roast (about 3 pounds), trimmed of fat

½ cup plus 2 tablespoons barbecue sauce, divided

¼ cup water

12 slider rolls

¾ cup prepared coleslaw

12 bread and butter pickle chips

Cut any roast larger than 2½ pounds in half so it cooks completely.

FAST

1. Coat inside of **CROCK-POT®** Express Crock Multi-Cooker with nonstick cooking spray. Combine brown sugar, cumin, chili powder, paprika, salt and ground red pepper in small bowl; toss to blend. Rub over roast; place in Express Crock. Pour in ½ cup barbecue sauce and water.

2. Secure lid. Press MEAT/STEW, set pressure to HIGH and time to 75 minutes. Make sure Steam Release Valve is in the "Seal" (closed) position. Press START/STOP.

3. Once cooking is complete, natural release pressure 10 minutes. Release remaining pressure. Remove roast to large bowl; shred with two forks. Remove 2 to 4 tablespoons liquid from Express Crock; add to shredded meat with remaining 2 tablespoons barbecue sauce. Arrange bottom half of rolls on platter or work surface. Top each with ¼ cup beef mixture, 1 tablespoon coleslaw and 1 pickle chip. Place roll tops on each.

---

1 tablespoon packed light brown sugar

1 teaspoon ground cumin

1 teaspoon chili powder

1 teaspoon paprika

½ teaspoon salt

¼ teaspoon ground red pepper

1 boneless beef bottom round roast (about 3 pounds), trimmed of fat

½ cup plus 2 tablespoons barbecue sauce, divided

¼ cup water

12 slider rolls

¾ cup prepared coleslaw

12 bread and butter pickle chips

Cut any roast larger than 2½ pounds in half so it cooks completely.

SLOW

1. Coat inside of **CROCK-POT®** Express Crock Multi-Cooker with nonstick cooking spray. Combine brown sugar, cumin, chili powder, paprika, salt and ground red pepper in small bowl; toss to blend. Rub over roast; place in Express Crock. Pour in ½ cup barbecue sauce and water.

2. Secure lid. Press SLOW COOK, set temperature and time to LOW 7 to 8 hours or to HIGH 4 to 5 hours. Make sure Steam Release Valve is in the "Release" (open) position. Press START/STOP.

3. Once cooking is complete, remove roast to large bowl; shred with two forks. Add 2 to 4 tablespoons liquid from Express Crock and remaining 2 tablespoons barbecue sauce to shredded meat; stir to blend. Arrange bottom half of rolls on platter or work surface. Top each with ¼ cup beef mixture, 1 tablespoon coleslaw and 1 pickle chip. Place roll tops on each.

SOUTHWEST-STYLE MEAT LOAF

MAKES 6 SERVINGS

FAST

2 cups water

1½ pounds ground beef

2 eggs

1 small onion, chopped (about ½ cup)

½ medium green bell pepper, chopped (about ½ cup)

½ cup plain dry bread crumbs

¾ cup chunky salsa, divided

1½ teaspoons ground cumin

¾ cup (3 ounces) shredded Mexican cheese blend

¾ teaspoon salt

¼ teaspoon black pepper

1. Place rack in **CROCK-POT®** Express Crock Multi-Cooker; add water. Combine beef, eggs, onion, bell pepper, bread crumbs, ¼ cup salsa, cumin, cheese, salt and black pepper in large bowl; mix well. Shape mixture into 7×5-inch oval. Prepare foil handles (page 13).

2. Tear off 18×12-inch piece of foil; fold in half crosswise to create 12×9-inch rectangle. Place meat loaf on foil; bring up sides of foil to create pan, leaving top of meat loaf uncovered. Top meat loaf with remaining ½ cup salsa. Place foil with meat loaf on rack using foil handles.

3. Secure lid. Press MEAT/STEW, set pressure to HIGH and time to 42 minutes. Make sure Steam Release Valve is in the "Seal" (closed) position. Press START/STOP.

4. Once cooking is complete, quick release pressure. Remove meat loaf to large cutting board using foil handles; discard foil. Let stand 10 minutes before slicing.

SLOW

2 cups water

1½ pounds ground beef

2 eggs

1 small onion, chopped (about ½ cup)

½ medium green bell pepper, chopped (about ½ cup)

½ cup plain dry bread crumbs

¾ cup chunky salsa, divided

1½ teaspoons ground cumin

¾ cup (3 ounces) shredded Mexican cheese blend

¾ teaspoon salt

¼ teaspoon black pepper

1. Place rack in **CROCK-POT®** Express Crock Multi-Cooker; add water. Combine beef, eggs, onion, bell pepper, bread crumbs, ¼ cup salsa, cumin, cheese, salt and black pepper in large bowl; mix well. Shape mixture into 7×5-inch oval. Prepare foil handles (page 13).

2. Tear off 18×12-inch piece of foil; fold in half crosswise to create 12×9-inch rectangle. Place meat loaf on foil; bring up sides of foil to create pan, leaving top of meat loaf uncovered. Top meat loaf with remaining ½ cup salsa. Place foil with meat loaf on rack using foil handles.

3. Secure lid. Press SLOW COOK, set temperature and time to LOW 7 to 8 hours or to HIGH 3 to 4 hours. Make sure Steam Release Valve is in the "Release" (open) position. Press START/STOP.

4. Once cooking is complete, remove meat loaf to large cutting board using foil handles; discard foil. Let stand 10 minutes before slicing.

BEEFY TORTILLA PIE

MAKES 4 TO 6 SERVINGS

2 teaspoons olive oil

1½ cups chopped onion

2 pounds ground beef

1 teaspoon salt

1 teaspoon ground cumin

1 teaspoon chili powder

2 cloves garlic, minced

1 can (15 ounces) tomato sauce

1 cup sliced black olives

1 cup water

8 (6-inch) flour tortillas

3½ cups (14 ounces) shredded Cheddar cheese

Optional toppings: sour cream, salsa and/or chopped green onions

1. Press BROWN/SAUTÉ on **CROCK-POT®** Express Crock Multi-Cooker; heat oil on HIGH. Add onion; cook and stir 3 to 5 minutes or until tender. Add beef, salt, cumin, chili powder and garlic; cook and stir 6 to 8 minutes or until beef is browned. Drain fat. Remove beef mixture to large bowl; stir in tomato sauce and olives.

2. Add water to Express Crock. Cover rack with foil; place in Express Crock. Prepare foil handles (page 13). Lay 1 tortilla on foil strips. Spread with meat sauce and ½ cup cheese. Top with another tortilla, meat sauce and cheese. Repeat layers five times, ending with tortilla. Secure lid. Press MEAT/STEW, set pressure to HIGH and time to 15 minutes. Make sure Steam Release Valve is in the "Seal" (closed) position. Press START/STOP.

3. Once cooking is complete, quick release pressure. Remove pie to large plate using foil handles. Discard foil. Cut into wedges. Serve with desired toppings.

2 teaspoons olive oil

1½ cups chopped onion

2 pounds ground beef

1 teaspoon salt

1 teaspoon ground cumim

1 teaspoon chili powder

2 cloves garlic, minced

1 can (15 ounces) tomato sauce

1 cup sliced black olives

1 cup water

8 (6-inch) flour tortillas

3½ cups (14 ounces) shredded Cheddar cheese

Optional toppings: sour cream, salsa and/or chopped green onions

1. Press BROWN/SAUTÉ on **CROCK-POT®** Express Crock Multi-Cooker; heat oil on HIGH. Add onion; cook and stir 3 to 5 minutes or until tender. Add beef, salt, cumin, chili powder and garlic; cook and stir 6 to 8 minutes or until beef is browned. Drain fat. Remove beef mixture to large bowl; stir in tomato sauce and olives.

2. Add water to Express Crock. Cover rack with foil; place in Express Crock. Prepare foil handles (page 13). Lay 1 tortilla on foil strips. Spread with meat sauce and ½ cup cheese. Top with another tortilla, meat sauce and cheese. Repeat layers five times, ending with tortilla. Secure lid. Press SLOW COOK, set temperature to HIGH and time to 1½ hours. Make sure Steam Release Valve is in the "Release" (open) position. Press START/STOP.

3. Once cooking is complete, remove pie from Express Crock using foil handles. Remove to large plate; discard foil. Cut into wedges. Serve with desired toppings.

HOT BEEF SANDWICHES AU JUS

MAKES 8 TO 10 SERVINGS

FAST

2 cans (about 10 ounces *each*) beef broth

1 can (12 ounces) beer

2 packages (1 ounce *each*) dry onion soup mix

1 tablespoon minced garlic

2 teaspoons sugar

1 teaspoon dried oregano

4 pounds boneless beef bottom round roast, trimmed*

Crusty French rolls, sliced in half

Cut any roast larger than 2¹/₂ pounds in half so it cooks completely.

1. Combine broth, beer, dry soup mix, garlic, sugar and oregano in **CROCK-POT®** Express Crock Multi-Cooker; stir to blend. Add beef. Secure lid. Press MEAT/STEW, set pressure to HIGH and time to 1 hour. Make sure Steam Release Valve is in the "Seal" (closed) position. Press START/STOP.

2. Once cooking is complete, natural release pressure 10 minutes. Release remaining pressure. Remove beef to large cutting board; shred with two forks. Return beef to cooking liquid; stir to blend. Serve on rolls with cooking liquid for dipping.

SLOW

2 cans (about 10 ounces *each*) beef broth

1 can (12 ounces) beer

2 packages (1 ounce *each*) dry onion soup mix

1 tablespoon minced garlic

2 teaspoons sugar

1 teaspoon dried oregano

4 pounds boneless beef bottom round roast, trimmed*

Crusty French rolls, sliced in half

Cut any roast larger than 2¹/₂ pounds in half so it cooks completely.

1. Combine broth, beer, dry soup mix, garlic, sugar and oregano in **CROCK-POT®** Express Crock Multi-Cooker; stir to blend. Add beef. Secure lid. Press SLOW COOK, set temperature to HIGH and time to 4 to 6 hours. Make sure Steam Release Valve is in the "Release" (open) position. Press START/STOP.

2. Once cooking is complete, remove beef to large cutting board; shred with two forks. Return beef to cooking liquid; stir to blend. Serve on rolls with cooking liquid for dipping.

CORNED BEEF AND CABBAGE

MAKES 6 SERVINGS

FAST

1 **corned beef brisket with seasoning packet (about 3 pounds)**

1 **cup water**

3 **to 5 slices bacon, chopped**

2 **onions, thickly sliced**

1 **head green cabbage, cut into wedges**

6 **medium potatoes, cut into wedges**

1 **package (8 to 10 ounces) baby carrots**

1. Place beef in bottom of **CROCK-POT®** Express Crock Multi-Cooker. Sprinkle with seasoning; pour in water. Secure lid. Press MEAT/STEW, set pressure to HIGH and time to 1 hour 30 minutes. Make sure Steam Release Valve is in "Seal" (closed) position. Press START/STOP.

2. Once cooking is complete, natural release pressure 10 minutes. Release remaining pressure. Remove beef to large cutting board; cover with foil. Reserve cooking liquid in medium bowl.

3. Press BROWN/SAUTÉ on Express Crock. Add bacon; cook and stir on HIGH until crisp. Remove to paper towel-lined plate using slotted spoon. Crumble bacon when cool enough to handle. Add onions to Express Crock with bacon drippings; cook 3 minutes or until softened. Skim off and discard fat from reserved liquid. Add cabbage, potatoes, carrots and reserved liquid to Express Crock. Secure lid. Press STEAM, set pressure to HIGH and time to 5 minutes.

4. Once cooking is complete, quick release pressure. Slice beef. Serve beef with vegetables; top with bacon and cooking liquid.

SLOW

3 **to 5 slices bacon, chopped**

2 **onions, thickly sliced**

1 **corned beef brisket with seasoning packet (about 3 pounds)**

1 **package (8 to 10 ounces) baby carrots**

6 **medium potatoes, cut into wedges**

1 **cup water**

1 **head green cabbage, cut into wedges**

1. Press BROWN/SAUTÉ on **CROCK-POT®** Express Crock Multi-Cooker. Add bacon; cook, uncovered, on HIGH until crisp. Remove to paper towel-lined plate. Set aside.

2. Place onions in bottom of Express Crock. Add corned beef with seasoning packet, carrots and potato wedges. Pour water over top. Secure lid. Press SLOW COOK, set temperature to LOW and time to 8 hours. Make sure Steam Release Valve is in the "Release" (open) position. Press START/STOP.

3. With 1 hour left in cooking time, add cabbage to Express Crock.

4. Once cooking is complete, serve corned beef with vegetables topped with bacon and cooking liquid.

SWEDISH MEATBALLS

MAKES 4 TO 6 SERVINGS

1½ pounds meat loaf mix (¾ pound beef and ¾ pound pork)

¼ cup plain dry bread crumbs

1 egg

1 teaspoon salt

1 teaspoon onion powder

1 teaspoon black pepper

¼ teaspoon ground allspice

1 cup beef broth

2 tablespoons Worcestershire sauce

2 tablespoons butter, melted

2 tablespoons all-purpose flour

¼ cup sour cream

1 tablespoon red currant jelly

Hot cooked noodles (optional)

Chopped fresh Italian parsley (optional)

1. Combine meat loaf mix, bread crumbs, egg, salt, onion powder, pepper and allspice in large bowl; shape mixture into 24 (1-inch) meatballs. Refrigerate 1 hour.

2. Combine broth and Worcestershire sauce in **CROCK-POT®** Express Crock Multi-Cooker; add meatballs. Secure lid. Press BEANS/CHILI, set pressure to HIGH and time to 8 minutes. Make sure Steam Release Valve is in the "Seal" (closed) position. Press START/STOP.

3. Once cooking is complete, quick release pressure. Remove meatballs to large bowl using slotted spoon. Press BROWN/SAUTÉ on Express Crock. Combine butter and flour in small bowl; stir to blend. Whisk half of butter mixture into Express Crock until well blended; repeat with remaining half. Combine sour cream and jelly in small bowl; stir to blend. Whisk half of jelly mixture into Express Crock until well blended; repeat with remaining half. Serve over noodles, if desired. Pour sauce over meatballs before serving. Garnish with parsley.

1½ pounds meat loaf mix (¾ pound beef and ¾ pound pork)

¼ cup plain dry bread crumbs

1 egg

1 teaspoon salt

1 teaspoon onion powder

1 teaspoon black pepper

¼ teaspoon ground allspice

1 cup beef broth

2 tablespoons Worcestershire sauce

2 tablespoons butter, melted

2 tablespoons all-purpose flour

¼ cup sour cream

1 tablespoon red currant jelly

Hot cooked noodles (optional)

Chopped fresh Italian parsley (optional)

1. Combine meat loaf mix, bread crumbs, egg, salt, onion powder, pepper and allspice in large bowl; shape mixture into 24 (1-inch) meatballs. Refrigerate 1 hour.

2. Combine broth and Worcestershire sauce in **CROCK-POT®** Express Crock Multi-Cooker; add meatballs. Secure lid. Press SLOW COOK, set temperature to HIGH and time to 5 hours. Make sure Steam Release Valve is in the "Release" (open) position. Press START/STOP.

3. Once cooking is complete, remove meatballs to large bowl using slotted spoon. Press BROWN/SAUTÉ on Express Crock. Combine butter and flour in small bowl; stir to blend. Whisk half of butter mixture into Express Crock until well blended; repeat with remaining half. Combine sour cream and jelly in small bowl; stir to blend. Whisk half of jelly mixture into Express Crock until well blended; repeat with remaining half. Pour sauce over meatballs. Serve over noodles, if desired. Garnish with parsley.

HONEY RIBS

MAKES 4 SERVINGS

FAST

- 3 tablespoons olive oil
- 2 pounds pork baby back ribs, trimmed and cut into 3- to 4-rib portions
- 1 can (about 14 ounces) beef broth
- ½ cup water
- 3 tablespoons soy sauce
- 2 tablespoons honey
- 2 tablespoons maple syrup
- 2 tablespoons barbecue sauce
- ½ teaspoon ground mustard
- Hot cooked corn (optional)

1. Press BROWN/SAUTÉ on **CROCK-POT®** Express Crock Multi-Cooker; heat oil on HIGH. Add ribs in batches; cook 5 to 7 minutes or until browned. Remove to large plate. Combine broth, water, soy sauce, honey, maple syrup, barbecue sauce and ground mustard in large bowl; stir to blend. Reserve half of sauce. Place remaining half of sauce and ribs in Express Crock.

2. Secure lid. Press MEAT/STEW, set pressure to HIGH and time to 30 minutes. Make sure Steam Release Valve is in the "Seal" (closed) position. Press START/STOP.

3. Once cooking is complete, natural release pressure 10 minutes. Release remaining pressure. Remove ribs to large bowl. Press BROWN/SAUTÉ on Express Crock; add reserved sauce. Cook, uncovered, on HIGH 10 to 12 minutes or until thickened. Serve ribs with sauce and corn, if desired.

SLOW

- 3 tablespoons olive oil
- 2 pounds pork baby back ribs, trimmed and cut into 3- to 4-rib portions
- 1 can (about 14 ounces) beef broth
- ½ cup water
- 3 tablespoons soy sauce
- 2 tablespoons honey
- 2 tablespoons maple syrup
- 2 tablespoons barbecue sauce
- ½ teaspoon ground mustard
- Hot cooked corn (optional)

1. Press BROWN/SAUTÉ on **CROCK-POT®** Express Crock Multi-Cooker; heat oil on HIGH. Add ribs in batches; cook 5 to 7 minutes or until browned. Remove to large plate. Combine broth, water, soy sauce, honey, maple syrup, barbecue sauce and ground mustard in large bowl; stir to blend. Reserve half of sauce. Place remaining half of sauce and ribs in Express Crock.

2. Secure lid. Press SLOW COOK, set temperature and time to LOW 6 to 8 hours or to HIGH 3 to 4 hours. Make sure Steam Release Valve is in the "Release" (open) position. Press START/STOP.

3. Once cooking is complete, remove ribs to large bowl. Press BROWN/SAUTÉ on Express Crock; add reserved sauce. Cook, uncovered, on HIGH 10 to 12 minutes or until thickened. Serve ribs with sauce and corn, if desired.

BONELESS PORK ROAST WITH GARLIC

MAKES 4 TO 6 SERVINGS

1 boneless pork loin roast (2 to 2½ pounds)

Salt and black pepper

3 tablespoons olive oil, divided

4 cloves garlic, minced

¼ cup chopped fresh rosemary

½ lemon, cut into ⅛- to ¼-inch slices

½ cup chicken broth

¼ cup dry white wine

1. Season pork with salt and pepper. Combine 2 tablespoons oil, garlic and rosemary in small bowl; stir to blend. Rub over pork. Roll and tie pork with kitchen string. Tuck lemon slices under string and into ends of roast.

2. Press BROWN/SAUTÉ on **CROCK-POT®** Express Crock Multi-Cooker; heat remaining 1 tablespoon oil on HIGH. Add pork; cook 6 to 8 minutes or until browned on all sides. Pour broth and wine over pork. Secure lid. Press MEAT/STEW, set pressure to HIGH and time to 20 minutes. Make sure Steam Release Valve is in the "Seal" (closed) position. Press START/STOP.

3. Once cooking is complete, natural release pressure 10 minutes. Release remaining pressure. Remove roast to large cutting board. Cover loosely with foil; let stand 10 to 15 minutes before removing kitchen string and slicing. Serve roast with cooking liquid.

1 boneless pork loin roast (2 to 2½ pounds)

Salt and black pepper

3 tablespoons olive oil, divided

4 cloves garlic, minced

¼ cup chopped fresh rosemary

½ lemon, cut into ⅛- to ¼-inch slices

½ cup chicken broth

¼ cup dry white wine

1. Season pork with salt and pepper. Combine 2 tablespoons oil, garlic and rosemary in small bowl; stir to blend. Rub over pork. Roll and tie pork with kitchen string. Tuck lemon slices under string and into ends of roast.

2. Press BROWN/SAUTÉ on **CROCK-POT®** Express Crock Multi-Cooker; heat remaining 1 tablespoon oil on HIGH. Add pork; cook 6 to 8 minutes or until browned on all sides. Pour broth and wine over pork. Secure lid. Press SLOW COOK, set temperature and time to LOW 8 to 9 hours or to HIGH 3½ to 4 hours. Make sure Steam Release Valve is in the "Release" (open) position. Press START/STOP.

3. Once cooking is complete, remove roast to large cutting board. Cover loosely with foil; let stand 10 to 15 minutes before removing kitchen string and slicing. Serve roast with cooking liquid.

CLASSIC BEEF AND NOODLES

MAKES 8 SERVINGS

FAST

1 tablespoon vegetable oil

2 pounds cubed beef stew meat

1½ cups beef broth

⅓ cup dry sherry

¼ pound mushrooms, sliced into halves

2 tablespoons chopped onion

2 cloves garlic, minced

1 teaspoon salt

1 teaspoon dried oregano

½ teaspoon black pepper

¼ teaspoon dried marjoram

1 whole bay leaf

1 container (8 ounces) sour cream

½ cup all-purpose flour

¼ cup water

4 cups hot cooked noodles

1. Press BROWN/SAUTÉ on **CROCK-POT®** Express Crock Multi-Cooker; heat oil on HIGH. Add beef in batches; cook 6 to 8 minutes or until browned on all sides. Drain fat. Wipe Express Crock clean.

2. Add beef, broth, sherry, mushrooms, onion, garlic, salt, oregano, pepper, marjoram and bay leaf to Express Crock; stir to blend. Secure lid. Press MEAT/STEW, set pressure to HIGH and time to 20 minutes. Make sure Steam Release Valve is in the "Seal" (closed) position. Press START/STOP.

3. Once cooking is complete, natural release pressure 10 minutes. Release remaining pressure. Remove and discard bay leaf. Press BROWN/SAUTÉ on Express Crock. Combine sour cream, flour and water in small bowl. Stir about 1 cup cooking liquid from Express Crock into sour cream mixture. Whisk mixture into Express Crock. Cook, uncovered, on HIGH 2 to 3 minutes or until thickened and bubbly. Serve over noodles.

SLOW

1 tablespoon vegetable oil

2 pounds cubed beef stew meat

1½ cups beef broth

⅓ cup dry sherry

¼ pound mushrooms, sliced into halves

2 tablespoons chopped onion

2 cloves garlic, minced

1 teaspoon salt

1 teaspoon dried oregano

½ teaspoon black pepper

¼ teaspoon dried marjoram

1 whole bay leaf

1 container (8 ounces) sour cream

½ cup all-purpose flour

¼ cup water

4 cups hot cooked noodles

1. Press BROWN/SAUTÉ on **CROCK-POT®** Express Crock Multi-Cooker; heat oil on HIGH. Add beef in batches; cook 6 to 8 minutes or until browned on all sides. Drain fat. Wipe Express Crock clean.

2. Add beef, broth, sherry, mushrooms, onion, garlic, salt, oregano, pepper, marjoram and bay leaf to Express Crock; stir to blend. Secure lid. Press SLOW COOK, set temperature and time to LOW 8 to 10 hours or to HIGH 4 to 5 hours. Make sure Steam Release Valve is in the "Release" (open) position. Press START/STOP.

3. Once cooking is complete, remove and discard bay leaf. Press BROWN/SAUTÉ on Express Crock. Combine sour cream, flour and water in small bowl. Stir about 1 cup cooking liquid from Express Crock into sour cream mixture. Whisk mixture into Express Crock. Cook, uncovered, on HIGH 2 to 3 minutes or until thickened and bubbly. Serve over noodles.

ITALIAN MEATBALL HOAGIES

MAKES 4 SERVINGS

FAST

- ½ pound ground beef
- ½ pound Italian sausage, casings removed
- ¼ cup seasoned dry bread crumbs
- ¼ cup grated Parmesan cheese, plus additional for topping
- 1 egg
- 1 cup pasta sauce
- ¼ teaspoon red pepper flakes (optional)
- 4 (6-inch) hoagie rolls, split
- Fresh chopped Italian parsley (optional)

1. Coat inside of **CROCK-POT®** Express Crock Multi-Cooker with nonstick cooking spray. Combine beef, sausage, bread crumbs, ¼ cup Parmesan cheese and egg in large bowl; mix well. Shape beef mixture into 16 (1½-inch) meatballs. Place meatballs in Express Crock in single layer. Pour pasta sauce over meatballs. Secure lid. Press MEAT/STEW, set pressure to HIGH and time to 15 minutes. Make sure Steam Release Valve is in "Seal" (closed) position. Press START/STOP.

2. Once cooking is complete, quick release pressure. Remove meatballs to medium bowl using slotted spoon; cover to keep warm. Press BROWN/SAUTÉ on Express Crock. Cook sauce, uncovered, on HIGH 5 to 10 minutes or until thickened. Return meatballs to Express Crock; toss to coat. Season with red pepper flakes, if desired. Serve meatballs and sauce in rolls; top with additional cheese.

SLOW

- ½ pound ground beef
- ½ pound Italian sausage, casings removed
- ¼ cup seasoned dry bread crumbs
- ¼ cup grated Parmesan cheese, plus additional for topping
- 1 egg
- 1 cup pasta sauce
- ¼ teaspoon red pepper flakes (optional)
- 4 (6-inch) hoagie rolls, split
- Fresh chopped Italian parsley (optional)

1. Coat inside of **CROCK-POT®** Express Crock Multi-Cooker with nonstick cooking spray. Combine beef, sausage, bread crumbs, ¼ cup Parmesan cheese and egg in large bowl; mix well. Shape mixture into 16 (1½-inch) meatballs. Place meatballs in Express Crock in single layer. Pour pasta sauce over meatballs. Secure lid. Press SLOW COOK, set temperature and time to LOW 5 to 7 hours or to HIGH 2½ to 3 hours. Make sure Steam Release Valve is in the "Release" (open) position. Press START/STOP.

2. Once cooking is complete, remove meatballs to medium bowl using slotted spoon; cover to keep warm. Press BROWN/SAUTÉ on Express Crock. Cook sauce, uncovered, on HIGH 5 to 10 minutes or until thickened. Return meatballs to Express Crock; toss to coat. Season with red pepper flakes, if desired. Serve meatballs and sauce in rolls; top with additional cheese.

BRISKET WITH SWEET ONIONS

MAKES 10 SERVINGS

FAST

2 tablespoons olive oil

1 flat-cut boneless beef brisket (about 3½ pounds)*

Salt and black pepper

2 large sweet onions, cut into 10 (½-inch) slices**

2 cans (about 14 ounces each) beef broth

1 teaspoon cracked black peppercorns

¾ cup crumbled blue cheese (optional)

*Cut any piece of meat larger than 2½ pounds in half so it cooks completely.
**Preferably Maui, Vidalia or Walla Walla onions.*

1. Press BROWN/SAUTÉ on **CROCK-POT®** Express Crock Multi-Cooker; heat oil on HIGH. Season brisket with salt and black pepper. Add brisket in batches; cook, uncovered, 8 minutes or until browned on all sides. Remove to large plate.

2. Add brisket, onions, broth and peppercorns to Express Crock. Secure lid. Press MEAT/STEW, set pressure to HIGH and time to 80 minutes. Make sure Steam Release Valve is in "Seal" (closed) position. Press START/STOP.

3. Once cooking is complete, natural release pressure 10 minutes. Release remaining pressure. Remove brisket to large cutting board; cover loosely with foil. Let stand 10 to 15 minutes. Remove onions to large serving platter using slotted spoon.

4. Press BROWN/SAUTÉ on Express Crock. Heat cooking liquid, uncovered, on HIGH 5 minutes or until reduced. Slice brisket; place on top of onions. Sprinkle with blue cheese, if desired. Serve with cooking liquid.

SLOW

2 tablespoons olive oil

1 flat-cut boneless beef brisket (about 3½ pounds)*

Salt and black pepper

2 large sweet onions, cut into 10 (½-inch) slices**

2 cans (about 14 ounces each) beef broth

1 teaspoon cracked black peppercorns

¾ cup crumbled blue cheese (optional)

*Cut any piece of meat larger than 2½ pounds in half so it cooks completely.
**Preferably Maui, Vidalia or Walla Walla onions.*

1. Press BROWN/SAUTÉ on **CROCK-POT®** Express Crock Multi-Cooker; heat oil on HIGH. Season brisket with salt and black pepper. Add brisket in batches; cook, uncovered, 8 minutes or until browned on all sides. Remove to large plate.

2. Add brisket, onions, broth and peppercorns to Express Crock. Secure lid. Press SLOW COOK, set temperature to HIGH and time to 6 hours. Make sure Steam Release Valve is in the "Release" (open) position. Press START/STOP.

3. Once cooking is complete, remove brisket to large cutting board; cover loosely with foil. Let stand 10 to 15 minutes. Remove onions to large serving platter using slotted spoon.

4. Press BROWN/SAUTÉ on Express Crock. Heat cooking liquid, uncovered, on HIGH 5 minutes or until reduced. Slice brisket; place on top of onions. Sprinkle with blue cheese, if desired. Serve with cooking liquid.

CHEESEBURGER POTATO CASSEROLE

MAKES 6 SERVINGS

FAST

- 1 **pound ground beef**
- 1/2 **cup chopped onion**
- 1 **can (about 10¾ ounces) Cheddar cheese soup**
- 1/4 **cup sweet pickle relish**
- 2 **tablespoons brown mustard**

- 2 **tablespoons ketchup, plus additional for topping**
- 1 **tablespoon Worcestershire sauce**
- 1 **cup water**

- 1 **package (30 ounces) shredded potatoes**
- 2 **cups (8 ounces) shredded Cheddar cheese**
- 1 **teaspoon salt**
- 1/2 **teaspoon black pepper**
- **Sliced green onions**

1. Press BROWN/SAUTÉ on **CROCK-POT®** Express Crock Multi-Cooker. Add beef and onion; cook, uncovered, on HIGH 6 to 8 minutes, stirring to break up meat. Remove beef mixture to large bowl using slotted spoon. Stir soup, relish, mustard, 2 tablespoons ketchup and Worcestershire sauce into beef mixture until well blended. Wipe Express Crock clean.

2. Place rack in Express Crock; add water. Spray 8-inch soufflé dish with nonstick cooking spray. Prepare foil handles (page 13). Arrange half of potatoes in bottom of prepared dish. Spoon half of meat mixture over potatoes. Sprinkle with 1½ cups cheese, ½ teaspoon salt and ¼ teaspoon pepper. Top with remaining half of potatoes. Add remaining half of beef mixture; sprinkle with remaining ½ cup cheese, ½ teaspoon salt and ¼ teaspoon pepper. Secure lid. Press MEAT/STEW, set pressure to HIGH and time to 30 minutes. Make sure Steam Release Valve is in the "Seal" (closed) position. Press START/STOP.

3. Once cooking is complete, quick release pressure. Top each serving with additional ketchup and green onions.

SLOW

- 1 **pound ground beef**
- 1/2 **cup chopped onion**
- 1 **can (about 10¾ ounces) Cheddar cheese soup**
- 1/4 **cup sweet pickle relish**
- 2 **tablespoons brown mustard**

- 2 **tablespoons ketchup, plus additional for topping**
- 1 **tablespoon Worcestershire sauce**
- 1 **cup water**

- 1 **package (30 ounces) shredded potatoes**
- 2 **cups (8 ounces) shredded Cheddar cheese**
- 1 **teaspoon salt**
- 1/2 **teaspoon black pepper**
- **Sliced green onions**

1. Press BROWN/SAUTÉ on **CROCK-POT®** Express Crock Multi-Cooker. Add beef and onion; cook, uncovered, on HIGH 6 to 8 minutes, stirring to break up meat. Remove beef mixture to large bowl using slotted spoon. Stir soup, relish, mustard, 2 tablespoons ketchup and Worcestershire sauce into beef mixture until well blended. Wipe Express Crock clean.

2. Place rack in Express Crock; add water. Spray 8-inch soufflé dish with nonstick cooking spray. Prepare foil handles (page 13). Arrange half of potatoes in bottom of prepared dish. Spoon half of meat mixture over potatoes. Sprinkle with 1½ cups cheese, ½ teaspoon salt and ¼ teaspoon pepper. Top with remaining half of potatoes. Add remaining half of beef mixture; sprinkle with remaining ½ cup cheese, ½ teaspoon salt and ¼ teaspoon pepper. Secure lid. Press SLOW COOK, set temperature and time to LOW 4 hours or to HIGH 2 hours. Make sure Steam Release Valve is in the "Release" (open) position. Press START/STOP.

3. Once cooking is complete, top with additional ketchup and green onions.

NACHO DIP

MAKES 10 CUPS

FAST

2 cups dried black beans, rinsed and sorted

3 cups water

2 tablespoons vegetable oil

1 onion, chopped

2 pounds ground beef

1 can (28 ounces) diced tomatoes

1 can (about 16 ounces) refried beans

1 can (about 15 ounces) cream-style corn

3 cloves garlic, minced

1 package (1¼ ounces) taco seasoning mix

Tortilla chips

Queso blanco

1. Place beans and water in **CROCK-POT®** Express Crock Multi-Cooker. Secure lid. Press BEANS/CHILI, set pressure to HIGH and time to 35 minutes. Make sure Steam Release Valve is in "Seal" (closed) position. Press START/STOP.

2. Once cooking is complete, natural release pressure 10 minutes. Release remaining pressure. Drain beans; set aside. Wipe Express Crock clean.

3. Press BROWN/SAUTÉ on Express Crock; heat oil on HIGH. Add onion; cook and stir 3 minutes or until softened. Add beef; cook 6 to 8 minutes or until browned, stirring to break up meat. Drain fat.

4. Stir beef mixture, black beans, tomatoes, refried beans, corn, garlic and taco seasoning mix into Express Crock; cook, uncovered, 5 to 7 minutes until heated through. Serve on tortilla chips. Sprinkle with queso blanco.

SLOW

1 tablespoon vegetable oil

1 onion, chopped

2 pounds ground beef

2 cans (about 15 ounces *each*) black beans, rinsed and drained

1 can (28 ounces) diced tomatoes

1 can (about 15 ounces) refried beans

1 can (about 15 ounces) cream-style corn

3 cloves garlic, minced

1 package (1¼ ounces) taco seasoning mix

Tortilla chips

Queso blanco

1. Press BROWN/SAUTÉ on **CROCK-POT®** Express Crock Multi-Cooker; heat oil on HIGH. Add onion; cook and stir 2 to 3 minutes or until softened. Add beef; cook 5 to 7 minutes or until browned, stirring to break up meat. Drain fat.

2. Stir beef mixture, black beans, tomatoes, refried beans, corn, garlic and taco seasoning mix into Express Crock. Secure lid. Press SLOW COOK, set temperature and time to LOW 5 to 6 hours or to HIGH 2½ to 3 hours. Make sure Steam Release Valve is in the "Release" (open) position. Press START/STOP.

3. Once cooking is complete, serve on tortilla chips. Sprinkle with queso blanco.

BARBECUE RIBS

MAKES 6 SERVINGS

3 tablespoons olive oil

2 racks pork baby back ribs, cut into individual rib sections

2 small red onions, finely chopped

3 to 4 cloves garlic, minced

1 cup packed brown sugar

1 cup ketchup

½ cup cider vinegar

Juice of 1 lemon

2 tablespoons Worcestershire sauce

1 tablespoon hot pepper sauce

½ teaspoon chili powder

1 cup beef broth

Sesame seeds (optional)

Chopped fresh thyme (optional)

FAST

1. Press BROWN/SAUTÉ on **CROCK-POT®** Express Crock Multi-Cooker; heat oil on HIGH. Add ribs in batches; cook, uncovered, 7 minutes or until browned. Remove ribs to large plate. Add onions and garlic to Express Crock; cook and stir 3 to 5 minutes or until softened. Stir in brown sugar, ketchup, vinegar, lemon juice, Worcestershire sauce, hot pepper sauce and chili powder; cook and stir 5 minutes. Remove half of sauce to large bowl; set aside.

2. Add ribs and broth to Express Crock; turn to coat. Secure lid. Press MEAT/STEW, set pressure to HIGH and time to 30 minutes. Make sure Steam Release Valve is in "Seal" (closed) position. Press START/STOP.

3. Once cooking is complete, natural release pressure 10 minutes. Release remaining pressure. Remove ribs to large bowl with reserved sauce; turn to coat. Skim fat from top of cooking liquid. Press BROWN/SAUTÉ on Express Crock; cook liquid, uncovered, on HIGH 5 to 7 minutes or until thickened. Serve sauce with ribs. Garnish ribs with sesame seeds and thyme.

3 tablespoons olive oil

2 racks pork baby back ribs, cut into individual rib sections

2 small red onions, finely chopped

3 to 4 cloves garlic, minced

1 cup packed brown sugar

1 cup ketchup

½ cup cider vinegar

Juice of 1 lemon

2 tablespoons Worcestershire sauce

1 tablespoon hot pepper sauce

½ teaspoon chili powder

Sesame seeds (optional)

Chopped fresh thyme (optional)

SLOW

1. Press BROWN/SAUTÉ on **CROCK-POT®** Express Crock Multi-Cooker; heat oil on HIGH. Add ribs in batches; cook, uncovered, 7 minutes or until browned. Remove ribs to large paper towel-lined plate. Add onions and garlic to Express Crock; cook and stir 3 to 5 minutes or until softened. Stir in brown sugar, ketchup, vinegar, lemon juice, Worcestershire sauce, hot pepper sauce and chili powder; cook and stir 5 minutes. Remove half of sauce to large bowl; set aside.

2. Add ribs to Express Crock; turn to coat. Secure lid. Press SLOW COOK, set temperature and time to LOW 7 to 9 hours or to HIGH 4 to 6 hours. Make sure Steam Release Valve is in the "Release" (open) position. Press START/STOP.

3. Once cooking is complete, remove ribs to large bowl with reserved sauce; turn to coat. Skim off and discard fat from cooking liquid. Press BROWN/SAUTÉ on Express Crock. Cook liquid, uncovered, on HIGH 5 to 7 minutes or until thickened. Serve sauce with ribs. Garnish ribs with sesame seeds and thyme.

ITALIAN-STYLE SAUSAGE WITH RICE

MAKES 4 TO 5 SERVINGS

FAST

- 1 pound mild Italian sausage links, cut into 1-inch pieces
- 1 can (about 15 ounces) pinto beans, rinsed and drained
- 1 cup pasta sauce
- 1 green bell pepper, cut into strips
- 1 small onion, halved and sliced
- ½ teaspoon salt
- ¼ teaspoon black pepper
- Hot cooked rice
- Fresh basil (optional)

1. Press BROWN/SAUTÉ on **CROCK-POT®** Express Crock Multi-Cooker. Brown sausage on HIGH 6 to 8 minutes, stirring to break up meat. Drain fat.

2. Combine sausage, beans, pasta sauce, bell pepper, onion, salt and black pepper in Express Crock. Press MEAT/STEW, set pressure to HIGH and time to 15 minutes. Make sure Steam Release Valve is in the "Seal" (closed) position. Press START/STOP.

3. Once cooking is complete, natural release pressure 10 minutes. Release remaining pressure. Serve with rice. Garnish with basil.

SLOW

- 1 pound mild Italian sausage links, cut into 1-inch pieces
- 1 can (about 15 ounces) pinto beans, rinsed and drained
- 1 cup pasta sauce
- 1 green bell pepper, cut into strips
- 1 small onion, halved and sliced
- ½ teaspoon salt
- ¼ teaspoon black pepper
- Hot cooked rice
- Fresh basil (optional)

1. Press BROWN/SAUTÉ on **CROCK-POT®** Express Crock Multi-Cooker. Brown sausage on HIGH 6 to 8 minutes, stirring to break up meat. Drain fat.

2. Combine sausage, beans, pasta sauce, bell pepper, onion, salt and black pepper in Express Crock. Secure lid. Press SLOW COOK, set temperature and time to LOW 4 to 6 hours or to HIGH 2 to 3 hours. Make sure Steam Release Valve is in the "Release" (open) position. Press START/STOP.

3. Once cooking is complete, serve with rice. Garnish with basil.

CARNITAS IN BELL PEPPERS

MAKES 4 SERVINGS

FAST

¹/₂ cup chicken broth

1 teaspoon salt

1 teaspoon minced garlic

¹/₂ teaspoon ground cumin

¹/₂ teaspoon dried oregano

¹/₂ teaspoon chili powder

¹/₂ teaspoon black pepper

2 pounds boneless pork roast

2 whole bay leaves

4 bell peppers (any color), halved

Optional toppings: guacamole, salsa and/or shredded Cheddar cheese

1. Coat inside of **CROCK-POT®** Express Crock Multi-Cooker with nonstick cooking spray; add broth.

2. Combine salt, garlic, cumin, oregano, chili powder and black pepper in small bowl; stir to blend. Rub salt mixture over pork; place pork and bay leaves in Express Crock. Secure lid. Press MEAT/STEW, set pressure to HIGH and time to 35 minutes. Make sure Steam Release Valve is in the "Seal" (closed) position. Press START/STOP.

3. Once cooking is complete, natural release pressure 10 minutes. Release remaining pressure. Remove pork to large cutting board; shred with two forks. Stir shredded pork back into Express Crock. Divide shredded pork evenly among bell peppers. Top as desired.

SLOW

¹/₂ cup chicken broth

1 teaspoon salt

1 teaspoon minced garlic

¹/₂ teaspoon ground cumin

¹/₂ teaspoon dried oregano

¹/₂ teaspoon chili powder

¹/₂ teaspoon black pepper

2 pounds boneless pork roast

2 whole bay leaves

4 bell peppers (any color), halved

Optional toppings: guacamole, salsa and/or shredded Cheddar cheese

1. Coat inside of **CROCK-POT®** Express Crock Multi-Cooker with nonstick cooking spray; add broth.

2. Combine salt, garlic, cumin, oregano, chili powder and black pepper in small bowl; stir to blend. Rub salt mixture over pork; place pork and bay leaves in Express Crock. Secure lid. Press SLOW COOK, set temperature to HIGH and time to 3¹/₂ hours. Make sure Steam Release Valve is in the "Release" (open) position. Press START/STOP.

3. Once cooking is complete, remove pork to large cutting board; shred with two forks. Stir shredded pork back into Express Crock. Divide shredded pork evenly among bell peppers. Top as desired.

SPICY SAUSAGE BOLOGNESE SAUCE

MAKES 6 SERVINGS

- 1 pound ground beef
- 1 pound hot Italian sausage, casings removed
- ¼ pound pancetta, diced
- 1 large onion, finely diced
- 2 medium carrots, finely diced
- 1 large stalk celery, finely diced
- ½ teaspoon salt
- ½ teaspoon black pepper
- 3 tablespoons tomato paste
- 1 tablespoon minced garlic
- 2 cans (28 ounces *each*) diced tomatoes, drained
- 1 cup dry red wine
- Hot cooked spaghetti (optional)
- Grated Parmesan cheese (optional)

1. Press BROWN/SAUTÉ on **CROCK-POT®** Express Crock Multi-Cooker. Add beef and sausage; cook, uncovered, on HIGH 6 to 8 minutes, stirring to break up meat. Remove to large bowl using slotted spoon. Add pancetta to Express Crock; cook and stir 5 minutes or until crisp and brown. Remove to small plate.

2. Add beef mixture, pancetta, onion, carrots, celery, salt and pepper to Express Crock; cook and stir 3 minutes or until vegetables are softened. Stir in tomato paste and garlic; cook and stir 1 minute. Stir in tomatoes and wine. Secure lid. Press MEAT/STEW, set pressure to HIGH and time to 20 minutes. Make sure Steam Release Valve is in "Seal" (closed) position. Press START/STOP.

3. Once cooking is complete, quick release pressure. Serve over pasta with cheese, if desired.

- 1 pound ground beef
- 1 pound hot Italian sausage, casings removed
- ¼ pound pancetta, diced
- 1 large onion, finely diced
- 2 medium carrots, finely diced
- 1 large stalk celery, finely diced
- ½ teaspoon salt
- ½ teaspoon black pepper
- 3 tablespoons tomato paste
- 1 tablespoon minced garlic
- 2 cans (28 ounces *each*) diced tomatoes, drained
- ¾ cup dry red wine
- Hot cooked spaghetti (optional)
- Grated Parmesan cheese (optional)

1. Press BROWN/SAUTÉ on **CROCK-POT®** Express Crock Multi-Cooker. Add beef and sausage; cook, uncovered, on HIGH 6 to 8 minutes, stirring to break up meat. Remove to large bowl using slotted spoon. Add pancetta; cook and stir 5 minutes or until crisp and brown. Remove to small plate.

2. Add beef mixture, pancetta, onion, carrots, celery, salt and pepper to Express Crock; cook and stir 3 minutes or until vegetables are softened. Stir in tomato paste and garlic; cook and stir 1 minute. Stir in tomatoes and wine. Secure lid. Press SLOW COOK, set temperature to LOW and time to 6 hours. Make sure Steam Release Valve is in the "Release" (open) position. Press START/STOP.

3. Once cooking is complete, serve over pasta with cheese, if desired.

APPLE-STUFFED PORK LOIN ROAST

MAKES 14 TO 16 SERVINGS

FAST

1 tablespoon butter

2 large tart apples, peeled, cored and thinly sliced (about 2 cups)

1 medium onion, cut into thin strips (about 1 cup)

2 tablespoons packed brown sugar

1 teaspoon Dijon mustard

2 cloves garlic, minced

1 teaspoon coarse salt

1 teaspoon dried rosemary

½ teaspoon dried thyme

½ teaspoon black pepper

1 boneless center cut pork loin roast (4 to 5 pounds)*

1 cup apple cider or apple juice

Cut any roast larger than 2½ pounds in half so it cooks completely.

1. Press BROWN/SAUTÉ on **CROCK-POT®** Express Crock Multi-Cooker. Add butter; heat on HIGH until melted. Add apples and onion; cook and stir 5 minutes or until soft. Stir in brown sugar and mustard. Remove to medium bowl. Wipe Express Crock clean.

2. Combine garlic, salt, rosemary, thyme and pepper in small bowl. Cut lengthwise down roast almost to, but not through, bottom. Open like a book. Rub half of garlic mixture onto cut sides of pork. Spread apple mixture evenly onto one cut side of roast. Close halves; tie roast with kitchen string at 2-inch intervals. Rub outside of roast with remaining garlic mixture.

3. Coat inside of Express Crock with nonstick cooking spray. Place roast in Express Crock; pour apple cider over roast. Secure lid. Press MEAT/STEW, set pressure to HIGH and time to 40 minutes. Make sure Steam Release Valve is in the "Seal" (closed) position. Press START/STOP.

4. Once cooking is complete, natural release pressure 10 minutes. Release remaining pressure. Remove roast to large cutting board. Cover loosely with foil; let stand 10 to 15 minutes before removing kitchen string and slicing. Serve roast with cooking liquid.

SLOW

1 tablespoon butter

2 large tart apples, peeled and thinly sliced (about 2 cups)

1 medium onion, cut into thin strips (about 1 cup)

2 tablespoons packed brown sugar

1 teaspoon Dijon mustard

2 cloves garlic, minced

1 teaspoon coarse salt

1 teaspoon dried rosemary

½ teaspoon dried thyme

½ teaspoon black pepper

1 boneless center cut pork loin roast (4 to 5 pounds)

1 cup apple cider or apple juice

Cut any roast larger than 2½ pounds in half so it cooks completely.

1. Press BROWN/SAUTÉ on **CROCK-POT®** Express Crock Multi-Cooker. Add butter; heat on HIGH until melted. Add apples and onion; cook and stir 5 minutes or until soft. Stir in brown sugar and mustard. Remove to medium bowl. Wipe Express Crock clean.

2. Combine garlic, salt, rosemary, thyme and pepper in small bowl. Cut lengthwise down roast almost to, but not through, bottom. Open like a book. Rub half of garlic mixture onto cut sides of pork. Spread apple mixture evenly onto one cut side of roast. Close halves; tie roast with kitchen string at 2-inch intervals. Rub outside of roast with remaining garlic mixture.

3. Coat inside of Express Crock with nonstick cooking spray. Place roast in Express Crock; pour apple cider over roast. Secure lid. Press SLOW COOK, set temperature and time to LOW 5 to 6 hours or to HIGH 2 to 3 hours. Make sure Steam Release Valve is in the "Release" (open) position. Press START/STOP.

4. Once cooking is complete, remove roast to large cutting board. Cover loosely with foil; let stand 10 to 15 minutes before removing kitchen string and slicing. Serve roast with cooking liquid.

CROCK AND GO HAM
WITH PINEAPPLE GLAZE

MAKES 6 TO 8 SERVINGS

FAST

1 **ham (about 3 pounds)**

10 **to 12 whole cloves**

1 **can (8 ounces) sliced pineapple, juice reserved and divided**

1 **jar (4 ounces) maraschino cherries plus 1 tablespoon juice, reserved and divided**

2 **tablespoons packed brown sugar**

1. Stud ham with cloves. Press BROWN/SAUTÉ on **CROCK-POT®** Express Crock Multi-Cooker. Add ham; cook on HIGH 4 to 5 minutes on each side until browned. Top with pineapple slices and cherries.

2. Combine reserved pineapple juice, brown sugar and reserved 1 tablespoon cherry juice in medium bowl; stir until glaze forms. Pour glaze over ham in Express Crock. Secure lid. Press MEAT/STEW, set pressure to HIGH and time to 20 minutes. Make sure Steam Release Valve is in the "Seal" (closed) position. Press START/STOP.

3. Once cooking is complete, natural release pressure 10 minutes. Release remaining pressure. Remove ham to large cutting board. Press BROWN/SAUTÉ on Express Crock. Heat cooking liquid, uncovered, on HIGH 3 minutes or until reduced. Remove cloves from ham before slicing. Serve with cooking liquid.

SLOW

1 **ham (3 pounds)**

10 **to 12 whole cloves**

1 **can (8 ounces) sliced pineapple, juice reserved and divided**

1 **jar (4 ounces) maraschino cherries plus 1 tablespoon juice, reserved and divided**

2 **tablespoons packed brown sugar**

1. Stud ham with cloves. Press BROWN/SAUTÉ on **CROCK-POT®** Express Crock Multi-Cooker. Add ham; cook on HIGH 4 to 5 minutes on each side until browned. Top with pineapple slices and cherries.

2. Combine reserved pineapple juice, brown sugar and reserved 1 tablespoon cherry juice in medium bowl; stir until glaze forms. Pour glaze over ham in Express Crock. Secure lid. Press SLOW COOK, set temperature to LOW and time to 6 to 8 hours. Make sure Steam Release Valve is in the "Release" (open) position. Press START/STOP.

3. Once cooking is complete, remove ham to large cutting board. Press BROWN/SAUTÉ on Express Crock. Heat cooking liquid, uncovered, on HIGH 3 minutes or until reduced. Remove cloves from ham before slicing. Serve with cooking liquid.

SWEET AND SPICY SAUSAGE ROUNDS

MAKES ABOUT 16 SERVINGS

FAST

1 **pound cooked kielbasa sausage, cut into ¼-inch-thick rounds**

⅔ **cup blackberry jam**

⅓ **cup steak sauce**

1 **tablespoon yellow mustard**

½ **teaspoon ground allspice**

½ **cup chicken broth**

1. Press BROWN/SAUTÉ on **CROCK-POT®** Express Crock Multi-Cooker. Add sausage; cook on HIGH 5 minutes or until browned.

2. Combine jam, steak sauce, mustard and allspice in medium bowl; stir to blend. Reserve half of sauce. Pour remaining half of sauce and broth over sausage in Express Crock. Secure lid. Press STEAM, set pressure to HIGH and time to 8 minutes. Make sure Steam Release Valve is in "Seal" (closed) position. Press START/STOP.

3. Once cooking is complete, quick release pressure. Remove sausage to large bowl with reserved sauce. Press BROWN/SAUTÉ on Express Crock; heat cooking liquid, uncovered, on HIGH 8 minutes or until reduced by half. Pour over sausage mixture; toss to coat.

SLOW

1 **pound kielbasa sausage, cut into ¼-inch-thick rounds**

⅔ **cup blackberry jam**

⅓ **cup steak sauce**

1 **tablespoon yellow mustard**

½ **teaspoon ground allspice**

1. Combine sausage, jam, steak sauce, mustard and allspice in **CROCK-POT®** Express Crock Multi-Cooker; stir to blend. Secure lid. Press SLOW COOK, set temperature to HIGH and time to 3 hours. Make sure Steam Release Valve is in the "Release" (open) position. Press START/STOP.

2. Once cooking is complete, serve sausage rounds from Express Crock using cocktail picks.

German Potato Salad
(page 194)

SIDE DISHES

LENTILS WITH WALNUTS

MAKES 4 TO 6 SERVINGS

FAST

1 cup dried brown lentils, rinsed and sorted

2 cups vegetable broth

1 small onion or large shallot, chopped

1 stalk celery, trimmed and chopped

1 large carrot, chopped

1/4 teaspoon dried thyme

Salt and black pepper

1/4 cup chopped walnuts

1. Combine lentils, broth, onion, celery, carrot, thyme, salt and black pepper in **CROCK-POT®** Express Crock Multi-Cooker. Secure lid. Press BEANS/CHILI, set pressure to HIGH and time to 10 minutes. Make sure Steam Release Valve is in "Seal" (closed) position. Press START/STOP.

2. Once cooking is complete, natural release pressure 10 minutes. Release remaining pressure. Remove lentils to serving bowls; sprinkle with walnuts.

SLOW

3 cups chicken broth

1 cup dried brown lentils, rinsed and sorted

1 small onion or large shallot, chopped

1 stalk celery, trimmed and chopped

1 large carrot, chopped

1/4 teaspoon dried thyme

Salt and black pepper

1/4 cup chopped walnuts

1. Combine broth, lentils, onion, celery, carrot, thyme, salt and pepper in **CROCK-POT®** Express Crock Multi-Cooker. Secure lid. Press SLOW COOK, set temperature to HIGH and time to 3 hours. Make sure Steam Release Valve is in the "Release" (open) position. Press START/STOP. (Lentils should absorb most or all of broth. Slightly tilt Express Crock to check.)

2. Once cooking is complete and most liquid is absorbed, season with salt and pepper. Spoon lentils into serving bowls and sprinkle with walnuts.

BBQ BAKED BEANS

MAKES 12 SERVINGS

FAST

4   slices bacon, chopped

1   package (16 ounces) dry cannellini beans, rinsed and sorted

4   cups chicken broth

³/₄   cup barbecue sauce

¹/₂   cup maple syrup

1¹/₂   teaspoons ground mustard

1. Press BROWN/SAUTÉ on **CROCK-POT®** Express Crock Multi-Cooker. Add bacon; cook, uncovered, on HIGH until crispy. Remove to small paper towel-lined plate.

2. Add beans and broth to Express Crock. Secure lid. Press BEANS/CHILI, set pressure to HIGH and time to 60 minutes. Make sure Steam Release Valve is in the "Seal" (closed) position. Press START/STOP.

3. Once cooking is complete, natural release pressure 10 minutes. Release remaining pressure. Add barbecue sauce, maple syrup and mustard; stir to blend. Beans will thicken more upon standing. Sprinkle each serving with bacon.

SLOW

3   cans (about 15 ounces *each*) cannellini beans, drained

4   slices bacon, chopped

³/₄   cup barbecue sauce

¹/₂   cup maple syrup

1¹/₂   teaspoons ground mustard

1. Coat inside of **CROCK-POT®** Express Crock Multi-Cooker with nonstick cooking spray. Add beans, bacon, barbecue sauce, maple syrup and mustard; stir to blend. Secure lid. Press SLOW COOK, set temperature to LOW and time to 4 hours. Make sure Steam Release Valve is in the "Release" (open) position. Press START/STOP.

2. Once cooking is complete, beans will thicken more upon standing.

HONEY-GLAZED CARROTS

MAKES 6 SERVINGS

FAST

8 **medium carrots (about 3 cups), cut diagonally into ⅛-inch slices**

½ **cup orange juice**

2 **tablespoons honey**

⅛ **teaspoon salt**

1. Coat inside of **CROCK-POT®** Express Crock Multi-Cooker with nonstick cooking spray. Combine carrots, orange juice, honey and salt in Express Crock; stir to blend. Secure lid. Press STEAM, set pressure to HIGH and time to 3 minutes. Make sure Steam Release Valve is in the "Seal" (closed) position. Press START/STOP.

2. Once cooking is complete, quick release pressure. Remove carrots to large serving bowl. Press BROWN/SAUTÉ on Express Crock; cook liquid, uncovered, on HIGH 5 minutes or until desired thickness. Pour liquid over carrots in serving bowl.

SLOW

8 **medium carrots (about 3 cups), cut diagonally into ⅛-inch slices**

½ **cup orange juice**

2 **tablespoons honey**

⅛ **teaspoon salt**

1. Coat inside of **CROCK-POT®** Express Crock Multi-Cooker with nonstick cooking spray. Combine carrots, orange juice, honey and salt in Express Crock; stir to blend. Secure lid. Press SLOW COOK, set temperature and time to LOW 4 hours or to HIGH 2½ hours. Make sure Steam Release Valve is in the "Release" (open) position. Press START/STOP.

2. Once cooking is complete, remove carrots to large serving bowl. Press BROWN/SAUTÉ on Express Crock; cook liquid, uncovered, on HIGH 5 minutes or until desired thickness. Pour liquid over carrots in serving bowl.

HARVARD BEETS

MAKES 6 SERVINGS

FAST

2 **pounds fresh beets, peeled and cut into 1-inch cubes**

1 **cup water**

²/₃ **cup sugar**

½ **cup cider vinegar**

1 **teaspoon salt**

1 **tablespoon cornstarch**

2 **tablespoons butter**

1. Combine beets, water, sugar, vinegar and salt in **CROCK-POT®** Express Crock Multi-Cooker; stir to blend. Secure lid. Press STEAM, set pressure to HIGH and time to 10 minutes. Make sure Steam Release Valve is in the "Seal" (closed) position. Press START/STOP.

2. Once cooking is complete, quick release pressure. Remove beets to large bowl using slotted spoon. Press BROWN/SAUTÉ on Express Crock; remove 2 tablespoons liquid to small bowl. Stir cornstarch into liquid until smooth; whisk into remaining cooking liquid. Stir in butter; cook, uncovered, on HIGH 2 minutes or until thickened. Pour sauce over beets.

SLOW

2 **pounds fresh beets, peeled and cut into 1-inch cubes**

²/₃ **cup sugar**

½ **cup cider vinegar**

¼ **cup water**

1 **teaspoon salt**

1 **tablespoon cornstarch**

2 **tablespoons butter**

1. Combine beets, sugar, vinegar, water and salt in **CROCK-POT®** Express Crock Multi-Cooker; stir to blend. Secure lid. Press SLOW COOK, set temperature to HIGH and time to 3 hours. Make sure Steam Release Valve is in the "Release" (open) position. Press START/STOP.

2. Once cooking is complete and beets are just tender, remove beets to large bowl using slotted spoon. Press BROWN/SAUTÉ on Express Crock; remove 2 tablespoons liquid to small bowl. Stir cornstarch into liquid until smooth; whisk into remaining cooking liquid. Stir in butter; cook, uncovered, on HIGH 2 minutes or until thickened. Pour sauce over beets.

CLASSIC SUCCOTASH

MAKES 8 SERVINGS

FAST

2 teaspoons olive oil

1 cup diced onion

1 cup diced green bell pepper

1 cup diced celery

1 can (about 14 ounces) diced tomatoes

1½ cups frozen corn

1½ cups frozen lima beans

1 tablespoon minced fresh Italian parsley

1 teaspoon paprika

Salt and black pepper

1. Press BROWN/SAUTÉ on **CROCK-POT®** Express Crock Multi-Cooker; heat oil on HIGH. Add onion, bell pepper and celery; cook and stir 5 minutes or until vegetables are tender. Stir in tomatoes, corn, beans, parsley, paprika, salt and black pepper. Secure lid. Press BEANS/CHILI, set pressure to HIGH and time to 3 minutes. Make sure Steam Release Valve is in the "Seal" (closed) position. Press START/STOP.

2. Once cooking is complete, quick release pressure. Remove to large serving bowl.

SLOW

2 teaspoons olive oil

1 cup diced onion

1 cup diced green bell pepper

1 cup diced celery

1 cup canned diced tomatoes

1½ cups frozen corn

1½ cups frozen lima beans

1 tablespoon minced fresh Italian parsley

1 teaspoon paprika

Salt and black pepper

1. Press BROWN/SAUTÉ on **CROCK-POT®** Express Crock Multi-Cooker; heat oil on HIGH. Add onion, bell pepper and celery; cook and stir 5 minutes or until vegetables are tender. Stir in tomatoes, corn, beans, parsley, paprika, salt and black pepper. Secure lid. Press SLOW COOK, set temperature and time to LOW 6 to 8 hours or to HIGH 3 to 4 hours. Make sure Steam Release Valve is in the "Release" (open) position. Press START/STOP.

2. Once cooking is complete, remove to large serving bowl.

BALSAMIC HONEY-GLAZED ROOT VEGETABLES

MAKES 6 SERVINGS

FAST

- 4 medium carrots, cut into ½-inch pieces
- 2 medium parsnips, cut into ¾-inch pieces
- 1½ pounds sweet potatoes, peeled and cut into 1-inch pieces
- 2 medium red onions, each cut through root end into 6 wedges
- ¼ cup honey
- 3 tablespoons unsalted butter, melted
- 1 tablespoon balsamic vinegar
- 1 teaspoon salt
- ¼ teaspoon black pepper

1. Combine carrots, parsnips, sweet potatoes, onions, honey, butter, vinegar, salt and pepper in **CROCK-POT®** Express Crock Multi-Cooker; toss to coat vegetables. Secure lid. Press STEAM, set pressure to HIGH and time to 5 minutes. Make sure Steam Release Valve is in the "Seal" (closed) position. Press START/STOP.

2. Once cooking is complete, quick release pressure. Remove vegetables to large bowl using slotted spoon. Press BROWN/SAUTÉ on Express Crock. Cook sauce, uncovered, 3 to 5 minutes or until desired thickness. Pour sauce over vegetables; toss to coat.

SLOW

- 4 medium carrots, cut into ½-inch pieces
- 2 medium parsnips, cut into ¾-inch pieces
- 1½ pounds sweet potatoes, peeled and cut into 1-inch pieces
- 2 medium red onions, each cut through root end into 6 wedges
- ¼ cup honey
- 3 tablespoons unsalted butter, melted
- 1 tablespoon balsamic vinegar
- 1 teaspoon salt
- ¼ teaspoon black pepper

1. Combine carrots, parsnips, sweet potatoes, onions, honey, butter, vinegar, salt and pepper in **CROCK-POT®** Express Crock Multi-Cooker; toss to coat vegetables. Secure lid. Press SLOW COOK, set temperature to LOW and time to 4 to 5 hours. Make sure Steam Release Valve is in the "Release" (open) position. Press START/STOP.

2. Once cooking is complete, remove vegetables to large bowl using slotted spoon. Press BROWN/SAUTÉ on Express Crock. Cook sauce, uncovered, 3 to 5 minutes or until desired thickness. Pour sauce over vegetables; toss to coat.

GARLIC AND HERB POLENTA

MAKES 6 SERVINGS

FAST

6 cups vegetable broth

2 cups corn grits

2 tablespoons butter

2 teaspoons salt

2 teaspoons finely minced garlic

3 tablespoons chopped fresh herbs such as parsley, chives, thyme or chervil (or a combination)

1. Coat inside of **CROCK-POT®** Express Crock Multi-Cooker with nonstick cooking spray. Add broth, corn grits, butter, salt and garlic; stir to blend. Secure lid. Press RICE/RISOTTO, set pressure to HIGH and time to 6 minutes. Make sure Steam Release Valve is in the "Seal" (closed) position. Press START/STOP.

2. Once cooking is complete, use natural release 5 minutes. Release remaining pressure. Stir in herbs just before serving.

SLOW

8 cups vegetable broth

2 cups corn grits

2 tablespoons butter

2 teaspoons finely minced garlic

2 teaspoons salt

3 tablespoons chopped fresh herbs such as parsley, chives, thyme or chervil (or a combination)

1. Coat inside of **CROCK-POT®** Express Crock Multi-Cooker with nonstick cooking spray. Add broth, corn grits, butter, garlic and salt; stir to blend. Secure lid. Press SLOW COOK, set temperature and time to LOW 4 hours or to HIGH 3 hours. Make sure Steam Release Valve is in the "Release" (open) position. Press START/STOP.

2. Once cooking is complete, stir in chopped herbs just before serving.

TOMATO TOPPING FOR BRUSCHETTA

MAKES 8 SERVINGS

FAST

- 6 medium tomatoes, peeled, seeded and diced
- 2 stalks celery, chopped
- 1/4 cup vegetable broth
- 2 shallots, chopped
- 4 pepperoncini peppers, chopped*
- 2 tablespoons olive oil
- 2 teaspoons tomato paste
- 1 teaspoon salt
- 1/2 teaspoon black pepper
- 8 slices country bread or other large round bread
- 2 cloves garlic, crushed

Pepperoncini are pickled peppers sold in jars with brine. They are available in the condiment aisle of large supermarkets.

1. Combine tomatoes, celery, broth, shallots, pepperoncini peppers, oil, tomato paste, salt and black pepper in **CROCK-POT®** Express Crock Multi-Cooker; stir gently to blend. Secure lid. Press STEAM, set pressure to HIGH and time to 3 minutes. Make sure Steam Release Valve is in "Seal" (closed) position. Press START/STOP.

2. Once cooking is complete, quick release pressure. Toast bread; immediately rub with garlic. Spread tomato topping on bread to serve.

SLOW

- 6 medium tomatoes, peeled, seeded and diced
- 2 stalks celery, chopped
- 2 shallots, chopped
- 4 pepperoncini peppers, chopped*
- 2 tablespoons olive oil
- 2 teaspoons tomato paste
- 1 teaspoon salt
- 1/2 teaspoon black pepper
- 8 slices country bread or other large round bread
- 2 cloves garlic, crushed

Pepperoncini are pickled peppers sold in jars with brine. They are available in the condiment aisle of large supermarkets.

1. Combine tomatoes, celery, shallots, pepperoncini peppers, oil, tomato paste, salt and black pepper in **CROCK-POT®** Express Crock Multi-Cooker; stir gently to blend. Secure lid. Press SLOW COOK, set temperature to LOW and time to 1 hour. Make sure Steam Release Valve is in the "Release" (open) position. Press START/STOP.

2. Once cooking is complete, toast bread; immediately rub with garlic. Spread tomato topping on bread to serve.

GERMAN POTATO SALAD

MAKES 6 SERVINGS

FAST

$\frac{1}{2}$ **pound bacon (about 8 slices), chopped**

1 **medium onion, chopped**

3 **stalks celery, chopped**

2 **pounds unpeeled small red potatoes, cut into $\frac{1}{4}$-inch slices**

1 **cup chicken broth**

$\frac{1}{4}$ **cup cider vinegar**

$\frac{1}{4}$ **teaspoon celery seed**

Salt and black pepper

1. Press BROWN/SAUTÉ on **CROCK-POT®** Express Crock Multi-Cooker. Add bacon; cook and stir on HIGH until bacon is crispy. Remove to paper towel-lined plate; set aside. Add onion and celery to bacon drippings in Express Crock; cook and stir 6 to 8 minutes or until onion is softened.

2. Stir potatoes into Express Crock; top with broth. Secure lid. Press STEAM, set pressure to HIGH and time to 6 minutes. Make sure Steam Release Valve is in the "Seal" (closed) position. Press START/STOP.

3. Once cooking is complete, quick release pressure. Stir in bacon, vinegar, celery seed, salt and pepper.

SLOW

$\frac{1}{2}$ **pound bacon (about 8 slices), chopped**

1 **medium onion, chopped**

3 **stalks celery, chopped**

2 **pounds unpeeled small red potatoes, cut into $\frac{1}{4}$-inch slices**

1 **cup chicken broth**

$\frac{1}{4}$ **cup cider vinegar**

$\frac{1}{4}$ **teaspoon celery seed**

Salt and black pepper

1. Press BROWN/SAUTÉ on **CROCK-POT®** Express Crock Multi-Cooker. Add bacon; cook and stir on HIGH until crispy. Remove bacon to paper towel-lined plate; set aside. Add onion and celery to bacon drippings in Express Crock; cook and stir 6 to 8 minutes or until onion is softened.

2. Stir in potatoes; top with broth. Secure lid. Press SLOW COOK, set temperature to HIGH and time to 4 hours. Make sure Steam Release Valve is in the "Release" (open) position. Press START/STOP.

3. Once cooking is complete, stir in bacon, vinegar, celery seed, salt and pepper.

CONFETTI BLACK BEANS

MAKES 6 SERVINGS

FAST

2 cups vegetable broth

1 cup dried black beans, rinsed and sorted

1½ teaspoons salt, divided

1 whole bay leaf

1 tablespoon olive oil

1 medium onion, chopped

1 cup chopped bell pepper (red, yellow, green or a combination)

1 jalapeño pepper, finely chopped*

2 cloves garlic, minced

1 large tomato, chopped

½ teaspoon ground cumin

½ teaspoon chili powder

⅛ teaspoon black pepper

Jalapeño peppers can sting and irritate the skin, so wear rubber gloves when handling peppers and do not touch your eyes.

1. Combine broth, beans, 1 teaspoon salt and bay leaf in **CROCK-POT®** Express Crock Multi-Cooker. Secure lid. Press BEANS/CHILI, set pressure to HIGH and time to 23 minutes. Make sure Steam Release Valve is in the "Seal" (closed) position. Press START/STOP.

2. Once cooking is complete, quick release pressure. Drain beans. Remove to medium bowl. Press BROWN/SAUTÉ on Express Crock; heat oil on HIGH. Add onion, bell peppers, jalapeño pepper and garlic; cook and stir 3 minutes or until vegetables are tender. Add tomato, cumin, chili powder, remaining ½ teaspoon salt and black pepper; cook and stir 1 minute. Stir in beans; mix well. Remove and discard bay leaf. Remove to large serving bowl.

SLOW

1 cup dried black beans, rinsed and sorted

1½ teaspoons olive oil

1 medium onion, chopped

¼ cup chopped red bell pepper

¼ cup chopped yellow bell pepper

1 jalapeño pepper, finely chopped*

1 large tomato, chopped

½ teaspoon salt

⅛ teaspoon black pepper

2 cloves garlic, minced

1 can (about 14 ounces) chicken broth

1 whole bay leaf

Jalapeño peppers can sting and irritate the skin, so wear rubber gloves when handling peppers and do not touch your eyes.

1. Place beans in large bowl and add enough cold water to cover by at least 2 inches. Soak 6 to 8 hours or overnight.** Drain beans. Remove to medium bowl.

2. Press BROWN/SAUTÉ on **CROCK-POT®** Express Crock Multi-Cooker; heat oil on HIGH. Add onion, bell peppers and jalapeño pepper; cook and stir 5 minutes or until onion is tender. Add tomato, salt and black pepper; cook 5 minutes. Stir in garlic.

3. Add beans, broth and bay leaf to Express Crock. Secure lid. Press SLOW COOK, set temperature to LOW 7 to 8 hours or to HIGH 4½ to 5 hours. Make sure Steam Release Valve is in the "Release" (open) position. Press START/STOP.

4. Once cooking is complete, remove and discard bay leaf.

**To quick soak beans, place beans in large saucepan; cover with water. Bring to a boil over high heat. Boil 2 minutes. Remove from heat; let soak, covered, 1 hour.

RED CABBAGE AND APPLES

MAKES 4 SERVINGS

1 **small head red cabbage, cored and thinly sliced**

1 **large apple, peeled and grated**

³/₄ **cup sugar**

½ **cup red wine vinegar**

1 **teaspoon ground cloves**

Fresh apple slices (optional)

1. Combine cabbage, grated apple, sugar, vinegar and cloves in **CROCK-POT®** Express Crock Multi-Cooker; stir to blend. Secure lid. Press STEAM, set pressure to HIGH and time to 6 minutes. Make sure Steam Release Valve is in the "Seal" (closed) position. Press START/STOP.

2. Once cooking is complete, natural release pressure 10 minutes. Release remaining pressure. Garnish with apple slices.

1 **small head red cabbage, cored and thinly sliced**

1 **large apple, peeled and grated**

³/₄ **cup sugar**

½ **cup red wine vinegar**

1 **teaspoon ground cloves**

Fresh apple slices (optional)

1. Combine cabbage, grated apple, sugar, vinegar and cloves in **CROCK-POT®** Express Crock Multi-Cooker. Secure lid. Press SLOW COOK, set temperature to HIGH and time to 6 hours. Make sure Steam Release Valve is in the "Release" (open) position. Press START/STOP.

2. Once cooking is complete, garnish with apple slices.

CANDIED SWEET POTATOES

MAKES 4 SERVINGS

FAST

3 **medium sweet potatoes (1½ to 2 pounds), peeled and sliced into ½-inch rounds**

1 **cup water**

¼ **cup (½ stick) butter, cut into small pieces**

2 **tablespoons sugar**

1 **tablespoon vanilla**

1 **teaspoon ground nutmeg**

1. Combine potatoes, water, butter, sugar, vanilla and nutmeg in **CROCK-POT®** Express Crock Multi-Cooker. Secure lid. Press STEAM, set pressure to HIGH and time to 5 minutes. Make sure Steam Release Valve is in the "Seal" (closed) position. Press START/STOP.

2. Once cooking is complete, quick release pressure. Remove potatoes to large serving bowl using slotted spoon.

SLOW

3 **medium sweet potatoes (1½ to 2 pounds), peeled and sliced into ½-inch rounds**

½ **cup water**

¼ **cup (½ stick) butter, cut into small pieces**

2 **tablespoons sugar**

1 **tablespoon vanilla**

1 **teaspoon ground nutmeg**

1. Combine potatoes, water, butter, sugar, vanilla and nutmeg in **CROCK-POT®** Express Crock Multi-Cooker. Secure lid. Press SLOW COOK, set temperature and time to LOW 7 hours or to HIGH 4 hours. Make sure Steam Release Valve is in the "Release" (open) position. Press START/STOP.

2. Once cooking is complete, remove potatoes to large serving bowl using slotted spoon.

GREEN BEAN CASSEROLE

MAKES 6 SERVINGS

FAST

2 pounds fresh green beans

1 can (10¾ ounces) condensed cream of mushroom soup, undiluted

½ cup water

1 tablespoon chopped fresh Italian parsley

1 tablespoon chopped roasted red peppers

1 teaspoon dried sage

½ teaspoon salt

½ teaspoon black pepper

¼ teaspoon ground nutmeg

½ cup toasted slivered almonds*

¼ teaspoon red pepper flakes (optional)

To toast almonds, spread in single layer in Express Crock. Press BROWN/SAUTÉ. Cook and stir on HIGH 1 to 2 minutes or until nuts are lightly browned. Remove from Express Crock immediately.

1. Combine beans, soup, water, parsley, red peppers, sage, salt, black pepper and nutmeg in **CROCK-POT®** Express Crock Multi-Cooker; stir to blend. Secure lid. Press STEAM, set pressure to HIGH and time to 3 minutes. Make sure Steam Release Valve is in the "Seal" (closed) position. Press START/STOP.

2. Once cooking is complete, quick release pressure. Sprinkle with almonds and red pepper flakes, if desired.

SLOW

2 pounds fresh green beans

1 can (10¾ ounces) condensed cream of mushroom soup, undiluted

1 tablespoon chopped parsley

1 tablespoon chopped roasted red peppers

1 teaspoon dried sage

½ teaspoon salt

½ teaspoon black pepper

¼ teaspoon ground nutmeg

½ cup toasted slivered almonds*

¼ teaspoon red pepper flakes (optional)

To toast almonds, spread in single layer in Express Crock. Press BROWN/SAUTÉ. Cook and stir on HIGH 1 to 2 minutes or until nuts are lightly browned. Remove from Express Crock immediately.

1. Combine beans, soup, parsley, red peppers, sage, salt, black pepper and nutmeg in **CROCK-POT®** Express Crock Multi-Cooker; stir to blend. Secure lid. Press SLOW COOK, set temperature to LOW and time to 3 to 4 hours. Make sure Steam Release Valve is in the "Release" (open) position. Press START/STOP.

2. Once cooking is complete, sprinkle each serving evenly with almonds and red pepper flakes, if desired.

CHEESY CORN AND PEPPERS

MAKES 8 SERVINGS

FAST

2 pounds frozen corn

2 poblano peppers, chopped

2 tablespoons butter, cubed

1 teaspoon salt

1/2 teaspoon ground cumin

1/4 teaspoon black pepper

3 ounces cream cheese, cubed

1 cup (4 ounces) shredded sharp Cheddar cheese

1. Coat inside of **CROCK-POT®** Express Crock Multi-Cooker with nonstick cooking spray. Combine corn, poblano peppers, butter, salt, cumin and black pepper in Express Crock; stir to blend. Secure lid. Press STEAM, set pressure to HIGH and time to 3 minutes. Make sure Steam Release Valve is in the "Seal" (closed) position. Press START/STOP.

2. Once cooking is complete, quick release pressure. Stir in cheeses until melted and creamy.

SLOW

2 pounds frozen corn

2 poblano peppers, chopped

2 tablespoons butter, cubed

1 teaspoon salt

1/2 teaspoon ground cumin

1/4 teaspoon black pepper

3 ounces cream cheese, cubed

1 cup (4 ounces) shredded sharp Cheddar cheese

1. Coat inside of **CROCK-POT®** Express Crock Multi-Cooker with nonstick cooking spray. Combine corn, poblano peppers, butter, salt, cumin and black pepper in Express Crock; stir to blend. Secure lid. Press SLOW COOK, set temperature to HIGH and time to 2 hours. Make sure Steam Release Valve is in the "Release" (open) position. Press START/STOP.

2. Once cooking is complete, stir in cheeses until melted.

QUINOA PILAF WITH SHALLOT VINAIGRETTE

MAKES 6 SERVINGS

1½ cups vegetable broth

1 cup uncooked quinoa, rinsed under cold running water

2 stalks celery, finely chopped

1 medium carrot, finely chopped

½ small red onion, finely chopped

¼ teaspoon dried thyme

1 medium shallot, chopped

1 tablespoon white wine vinegar

2 teaspoons honey

1 teaspoon Dijon mustard

⅛ teaspoon black pepper

¼ cup extra virgin olive oil

Chopped fresh Italian parsley (optional)

1. Combine broth, quinoa, celery, carrot, onion and thyme in **CROCK-POT®** Express Crock Multi-Cooker. Press RICE/RISOTTO, set pressure to LOW and time to 12 minutes. Make sure Steam Release Valve is in the "Seal" (closed) position. Press START/STOP.

2. Meanwhile, combine shallot, vinegar, honey, mustard and pepper in small bowl; whisk in oil.

3. Once cooking is complete, natural release pressure 10 minutes. Release remaining pressure. Fluff quinoa with fork; stir in shallot mixture. Garnish with parsley.

2 cups vegetable broth

1 cup uncooked quinoa, rinsed under cold running water

2 stalks celery, finely chopped

1 carrot, finely chopped

½ small red onion, finely chopped

¼ teaspoon dried thyme

1 medium shallot, chopped

1 tablespoon white wine vinegar

2 teaspoons honey

1 teaspoon Dijon mustard

⅛ teaspoon black pepper

¼ cup extra virgin olive oil

Chopped fresh Italian parsley (optional)

1. Combine broth, quinoa, celery, carrot, onion and thyme in **CROCK-POT®** Express Crock Multi-Cooker. Secure lid. Press SLOW COOK, set temperature to HIGH and time to 2 to 3 hours. Make sure Steam Release Valve is in the "Release" (open) position. Press START/STOP.

2. Meanwhile, combine shallot, vinegar, honey, mustard and pepper in small bowl; whisk in oil.

3. Once cooking is complete and liquid is absorbed, fluff quinoa with fork. Stir shallot mixture into quinoa; garnish with parsley.

BRUSSELS SPROUTS WITH BACON, THYME AND RAISINS

MAKES 8 SERVINGS

FAST

2 **thick slices applewood smoked bacon, chopped**

2 **pounds Brussels sprouts, ends trimmed and cut in half lengthwise**

½ **cup chicken broth**

⅔ **cup golden raisins**

2 **tablespoons chopped fresh thyme**

1. Press BROWN/SAUTÉ on **CROCK-POT®** Express Crock Multi-Cooker. Add bacon; cook and stir on HIGH until crisp. Remove to small paper towel-lined plate using slotted spoon. Crumble and set aside. Reserve drippings.

2. Combine sprouts, broth, raisins and thyme with bacon drippings in Express Crock; stir to blend. Secure lid. Press STEAM, set pressure to HIGH and time to 5 minutes. Make sure Steam Release Valve is in the "Seal" (closed) position. Press START/STOP.

3. Once cooking is complete, quick release pressure. Top each serving with reserved bacon.

SLOW

2 **thick slices applewood smoked bacon, chopped**

2 **pounds Brussels sprouts, ends trimmed and cut in half lengthwise**

1 **cup chicken broth**

⅔ **cup golden raisins**

2 **tablespoons chopped fresh thyme**

1. Press BROWN/SAUTÉ on **CROCK-POT®** Express Crock Multi-Cooker. Add bacon; cook and stir on HIGH until crisp. Remove to small paper towel-lined plate using slotted spoon. Crumble and set aside. Reserve drippings.

2. Combine sprouts, broth, raisins and thyme with bacon drippings in Express Crock; stir to blend. Secure lid. Press SLOW COOK, set temperature to LOW and time to 3 to 4 hours. Make sure Steam Release Valve is in the "Release" (open) position. Press START/STOP.

3. Once cooking is complete, top each serving with reserved bacon.

MUSHROOM WILD RICE

MAKES 8 SERVINGS

1 cup vegetable broth

1 cup uncooked wild rice

1/2 cup diced onion

1/2 cup sliced mushrooms

1/2 cup diced red or green bell pepper

Salt and black pepper

1. Combine broth, rice, onion, mushrooms, bell pepper, salt and black pepper in **CROCK-POT®** Express Crock Multi-Cooker; stir to blend. Secure lid. Press RICE/RISOTTO, set pressure to LOW and time to 12 minutes. Make sure Steam Release Valve is in the "Seal" (closed) position. Press START/STOP.

2. Once cooking is complete, natural release pressure 10 minutes. Release remaining pressure. Remove to large serving bowl.

1 1/2 cups vegetable broth

1 cup uncooked wild rice

1/2 cup diced onion

1/2 cup sliced mushrooms

1/2 cup diced red or green bell pepper

Salt and black pepper

1. Combine broth, rice, onion, mushrooms, bell pepper, salt and black pepper in **CROCK-POT®** Express Crock Multi-Cooker; stir to blend. Secure lid. Press SLOW COOK, set temperature to HIGH and time to 2 1/2 hours. Make sure Steam Release Valve is in the "Release" (open) position. Press START/STOP.

2. Once cooking is complete, rice is tender and liquid is absorbed, remove to large serving bowl.

BRAISED CABBAGE

MAKES 6 SERVINGS

3 slices bacon

1 head (about 3 pounds) green cabbage, cut into 1-inch-thick wedges

1 medium red onion, thinly sliced

1½ cups chicken broth

2 tablespoons unsalted butter, cubed

Salt and black pepper

1. Press BROWN/SAUTÉ on **CROCK-POT®** Express Crock Multi-Cooker. Add bacon; cook and stir on HIGH until crisp. Remove to paper towel-lined plate using slotted spoon; crumble. Set aside.

2. Layer cabbage and onion in Express Crock with bacon drippings. Pour in broth; top with butter. Secure lid. Press STEAM, set pressure to HIGH and time to 6 minutes. Make sure Steam Release Valve is in "Seal" (closed) position. Press START/STOP.

3. Once cooking is complete, quick release pressure. Sprinkle cabbage with crumbled bacon, salt and pepper just before serving.

3 slices bacon

1 head (about 3 pounds) green cabbage, cut into 1-inch-thick wedges

1 medium red onion, thinly sliced

3 cups chicken broth

2 tablespoons unsalted butter, cubed

Salt and black pepper

1. Press BROWN/SAUTÉ on **CROCK-POT®** Express Crock Multi-Cooker. Add bacon; cook and stir on HIGH until crisp. Remove to paper towel-lined plate using slotted spoon; crumble. Set aside.

2. Layer cabbage and onion in Express Crock. Pour in broth; top with butter. Secure lid. Press SLOW COOK, set temperature and time to LOW 6 to 7 hours or to HIGH 3 to 4 hours. Make sure Steam Release Valve is in the "Release" (open) position. Press START/STOP.

3. Once cooking is complete and cabbage is tender, sprinkle cabbage with crumbled bacon, salt and pepper just before serving.

Vanilla Sour Cream Cheesecake
(page 232)

SWEET TREATS

ENGLISH BREAD PUDDING

MAKES 6 SERVINGS

FAST

1½ cups water

8 ounces stale bread, cut into 1-inch pieces

1 cup chopped apple

¾ cup mixed dried fruit (raisins, cranberries, dates, etc.)

¼ cup chopped walnuts

1¾ cups milk

2 eggs

¼ cup packed brown sugar

2 tablespoons butter, melted

½ teaspoon ground cinnamon

⅛ teaspoon ground nutmeg

Pinch ground cloves

Pinch salt

Apple slices (optional)

1. Spray 6- to 7-inch (1½-quart) soufflé dish or round baking dish that fits inside **CROCK-POT®** Express Crock Multi-Cooker with nonstick cooking spray. Prepare foil handles (page 13). Place rack in Express Crock; add water.

2. Combine bread, chopped apples, dried fruit and nuts in medium bowl. Whisk milk, eggs, brown sugar, butter, cinnamon, nutmeg, cloves and salt in another medium bowl. Pour over bread mixture; stir to coat. Let stand 15 minutes, stirring occasionally.

3. Remove bread mixture to prepared dish; cover with foil. Place dish on rack using foil handles. Secure lid. Press DESSERT, set pressure to HIGH and time to 45 minutes. Make sure Steam Release Valve is in the "Seal" (closed) position. Press START/STOP.

4. Once cooking is complete, use natural release 10 minutes. Release remaining pressure. Garnish each serving with apple slices.

SLOW

1½ cups water

8 ounces stale bread, cut into 1-inch pieces

1 cup chopped apple

¾ cup mixed dried fruit (raisins, cranberries, dates, etc.)

¼ cup chopped walnuts

1¼ cups milk

2 eggs

¼ cup packed brown sugar

2 tablespoons butter, melted

½ teaspoon ground cinnamon

⅛ teaspoon ground nutmeg

Pinch ground cloves

Pinch salt

Apple slices (optional)

1. Spray 6- to 7-inch (1½-quart) soufflé dish or round baking dish that fits inside **CROCK-POT®** Express Crock Multi-Cooker with nonstick cooking spray. Prepare foil handles (page 13). Place rack in Express Crock; add water.

2. Combine bread, chopped apples, dried fruit and nuts in medium bowl. Whisk milk, eggs, brown sugar, butter, cinnamon, nutmeg, cloves and salt in another medium bowl. Pour over bread mixture; stir to coat. Let stand 15 minutes, stirring occasionally.

3. Remove bread mixture to prepared dish; cover with foil. Place dish on rack using foil handles. Secure lid. Press SLOW COOK, set temperature to LOW and time to 3½ to 4 hours. Make sure Steam Release Valve is in the "Release" (open) position. Press START/STOP.

4. Once cooking is complete and toothpick inserted into center of pudding comes out clean, garnish each serving with apple slices.

FRUIT AND NUT BAKED APPLES

MAKES 4 SERVINGS

- 4 **large baking apples, such as Rome Beauty or Jonathan**
- 1 **tablespoon lemon juice**
- 1/3 **cup chopped dried apricots**
- 1/3 **cup chopped walnuts or pecans**
- 3 **tablespoons packed brown sugar**
- 1/2 **teaspoon ground cinnamon**
- 2 **tablespoons unsalted butter, melted**
- 1/2 **cup water**

Caramel topping (optional)

1. Scoop out center of each apple, leaving 1 1/2-inch-wide cavity about 1/2 inch from bottom. Peel top of apple down about 1 inch. Brush peeled edges evenly with lemon juice. Combine apricots, walnuts, brown sugar and cinnamon in small bowl; stir to blend. Add butter; mix well. Spoon mixture evenly into apple cavities.

2. Pour water in bottom of **CROCK-POT®** Express Crock Multi-Cooker. Place rack in Express Crock. Place apples on rack. Secure lid. Press STEAM, set pressure to HIGH and time to 3 minutes. Make sure Steam Release Valve is in the "Seal" (closed) position. Press START/STOP.

3. Once cooking is complete, quick release pressure. Serve warm or at room temperature with caramel topping, if desired.

- 4 **large baking apples, such as Rome Beauty or Jonathan**
- 1 **tablespoon lemon juice**
- 1/3 **cup chopped dried apricots**
- 1/3 **cup chopped walnuts or pecans**
- 3 **tablespoons packed brown sugar**
- 1/2 **teaspoon ground cinnamon**
- 2 **tablespoons unsalted butter, melted**
- 1/2 **cup water**

Caramel topping (optional)

1. Scoop out center of each apple, leaving 1 1/2-inch-wide cavity about 1/2 inch from bottom. Peel top of apple down about 1 inch. Brush peeled edges evenly with lemon juice. Combine apricots, walnuts, brown sugar and cinnamon in small bowl; stir to blend. Add butter; mix well. Spoon mixture evenly into apple cavities.

2. Pour water in bottom of **CROCK-POT®** Express Crock Multi-Cooker. Place rack in Express Crock. Place apples on rack. Secure lid. Press SLOW COOK, set temperature to LOW and time to 3 to 4 hours. Make sure Steam Release Valve is in the "Release" (open) position. Press START/STOP.

3. Once cooking is complete, serve warm or at room temperature with caramel topping, if desired.

HAWAIIAN BREAD FRENCH TOAST

MAKES 8 TO 10 SERVINGS

FAST

- 2 tablespoons unsalted butter, cut into ¼-inch pieces, plus additional for soufflé dish and foil
- 1 cup water
- 1 pound sliced sweet Hawaiian rolls or bread, sliced lengthwise
- 6 eggs
- 1 cup milk
- 1 cup whipping cream
- ¼ cup sugar
- 2 teaspoons coconut extract
- 2 teaspoons vanilla
- 1 teaspoon ground cinnamon
- ½ cup flaked coconut, toasted*

To toast coconut, spread in single layer in Express Crock. Press BROWN/SAUTÉ. Cook and stir on HIGH 1 to 2 minutes or until lightly browned. Remove from Express Crock immediately.

1. Butter 8-inch (2-quart) soufflé dish or round baking dish that fits inside of **CROCK-POT®** Express Crock Multi-Cooker. Prepare foil handles (page 13). Place rack in Express Crock; add water.

2. Arrange bread in prepared dish; sprinkle with 2 tablespoons butter. Whisk eggs, milk, cream, sugar, coconut extract, vanilla and cinnamon in large bowl; pour over bread. Press bread into liquid. Set aside 10 minutes or until liquid is absorbed. Cover dish with buttered foil; buttered side down.

3. Place prepared dish on rack using foil handles. Secure lid. Press DESSERT, set pressure to HIGH and time to 45 minutes. Make sure Steam Release Valve is in the "Seal" (closed) position. Press START/STOP.

4. Once cooking is complete, natural release pressure 10 minutes. Release remaining pressure. Remove dish using foil handles; let stand 10 minutes. Sprinkle with coconut.

SLOW

- 2 tablespoons unsalted butter, cut into ¼-inch pieces, plus additional for soufflé dish and foil
- 1 cup water
- 1 pound sliced sweet Hawaiian rolls or bread, sliced lengthwise
- 6 eggs
- 1 cup milk
- 1 cup whipping cream
- ¼ cup sugar
- 2 teaspoons coconut extract
- 2 teaspoons vanilla
- 1 teaspoon ground cinnamon
- ½ cup flaked coconut, toasted*

To toast coconut, spread in single layer in Express Crock. Press BROWN/SAUTÉ. Cook and stir on HIGH 1 to 2 minutes or until lightly browned. Remove from Express Crock immediately.

1. Butter 8-inch (2-quart) soufflé dish or round baking dish that fits inside of **CROCK-POT®** Express Crock Multi-Cooker. Prepare foil handles (page 13). Place rack in Express Crock; add water.

2. Arrange bread in prepared dish; sprinkle with butter. Whisk eggs, milk, cream, sugar, coconut extract, vanilla and cinnamon in large bowl; pour over bread. Press bread into liquid. Set aside 10 minutes or until liquid is absorbed. Cover dish with buttered foil; buttered side down.

3. Place prepared dish on rack using foil handles. Secure lid. Press SLOW COOK, set temperature to HIGH and time to 2 hours. Make sure Steam Release Valve is in the "Release" (open) position. Press START/STOP.

4. Once cooking is complete, remove dish using foil handles; let stand 10 minutes. Sprinkle with coconut.

FIGS POACHED IN RED WINE

MAKES 4 SERVINGS

1 cup dry red wine

1 cup packed brown sugar

12 dried Calimyrna or Mediterranean figs (about 6 ounces)

2 (3-inch) whole cinnamon sticks

1 teaspoon finely grated orange peel

4 tablespoons whipping cream (optional)

1. Combine wine, brown sugar, figs, cinnamon sticks and orange peel in **CROCK-POT®** Express Crock Multi-Cooker; stir to blend. Secure lid. Press STEAM, set pressure to HIGH and time to 5 minutes. Make sure Steam Release Valve is in the "Seal" (closed) position. Press START/STOP.

2. Once cooking is complete, quick release pressure. Remove and discard cinnamon sticks. Remove figs to medium bowl using slotted spoon. Press BROWN/SAUTÉ on Express Crock; cook syrup, uncovered, on HIGH 5 minutes or until reduced by half. Spoon syrup and cream, if desired, into serving dishes; top with figs.

1 cup dry red wine

1 cup packed brown sugar

12 dried Calimyrna or Mediterranean figs (about 6 ounces)

2 (3-inch) whole cinnamon sticks

1 teaspoon finely grated orange peel

4 tablespoons whipping cream (optional)

1. Combine wine, brown sugar, figs, cinnamon sticks and orange peel in **CROCK-POT®** Express Crock Multi-Cooker; stir to blend. Secure lid. Press SLOW COOK, set temperature and time to LOW 5 to 6 hours or to HIGH 4 to 5 hours. Make sure Steam Release Valve is in the "Release" (open) position. Press START/STOP.

2. Once cooking is complete, remove and discard cinnamon sticks. Remove figs to medium bowl using slotted spoon. Press BROWN/SAUTÉ on Express Crock; cook syrup, uncovered, on HIGH 5 minutes or until reduced by half. Spoon syrup and cream, if desired, into serving dishes; top with figs.

PINEAPPLE RICE PUDDING

MAKES 8 SERVINGS

1½ cups water

¾ cup uncooked Arborio rice

¼ teaspoon salt

1 can (20 ounces) crushed pineapple in juice, undrained

1 can (13½ ounces) unsweetened coconut milk

1 can (12 ounces) evaporated milk

2 eggs, lightly beaten

¼ cup granulated sugar

¼ cup packed brown sugar

½ teaspoon ground cinnamon

¼ teaspoon ground nutmeg

Toasted coconut (optional)*

Pineapple slices (optional)

To toast coconut, spread in single layer in Express Crock. Press BROWN/SAUTÉ on Express Crock. Cook and stir on HIGH 1 to 2 minutes or until lightly browned. Remove from Express Crock immediately.

1. Combine water, rice and salt in **CROCK-POT®** Express Crock Multi-Cooker; stir to blend. Secure lid. Press RICE/RISOTTO, set pressure to HIGH and time to 6 minutes. Make sure Steam Release Valve is in the "Seal" (closed) position. Press START/STOP.

2. Once cooking is complete, natural release pressure 10 minutes. Release remaining pressure. Combine crushed pineapple, coconut milk, evaporated milk, eggs, sugars, cinnamon and nutmeg in large bowl; stir to blend. Stir pineapple mixture into cooked rice. Press BROWN/SAUTÉ on Express Crock; cook, uncovered, on HIGH 13 to 15 minutes or until thickened. Remove immediately to serving dishes. Garnish with toasted coconut and pineapple slices.

1½ cups water

¼ cup uncooked Arborio rice

¼ teaspoon salt

1 can (20 ounces) crushed pineapple in juice, undrained

1 can (13½ ounces) unsweetened coconut milk

1 can (12 ounces) evaporated milk

2 eggs, lightly beaten

¼ cup granulated sugar

¼ cup packed brown sugar

½ teaspoon ground cinnamon

¼ teaspoon ground nutmeg

Toasted coconut (optional)*

Pineapple slices (optional)

To toast coconut, spread in single layer in Express Crock. Press BROWN/SAUTÉ on Express Crock. Cook and stir on HIGH 1 to 2 minutes or until lightly browned. Remove from Express Crock immediately.

1. Combine water, rice and salt in **CROCK-POT®** Express Crock Multi-Cooker; stir to blend. Secure lid. Press SLOW COOK, set temperature to HIGH and time to 3 to 4 hours. Make sure Steam Release Valve is in the "Release" (open) position. Press START/STOP.

2. Once cooking is complete and rice is tender, combine crushed pineapple, coconut milk, evaporated milk, eggs, sugars, cinnamon and nutmeg in large bowl; stir to blend. Stir pineapple mixture into cooked rice. Press BROWN/SAUTÉ on Express Crock; cook, uncovered, on HIGH 13 to 15 minutes or until thickened. Remove immediately to serving dishes. Garnish with toasted coconut and pineapple slices.

FRUIT-TOPPED CHOCOLATE OATMEAL

MAKES 8 SERVINGS

4 **cups water**

2 **cups old-fashioned oats**

¼ **cup sugar**

2 **tablespoons unsweetened cocoa powder**

2 **cups fresh pitted cherries or frozen dark sweet cherries**

2 **cans (11 ounces *each*) mandarin orange segments in light syrup, rinsed and drained**

1. Combine water, oats, sugar and cocoa in **CROCK-POT®** Express Crock Multi-Cooker; stir to blend. Secure lid. Press STEAM, set pressure to HIGH and time to 8 minutes. Make sure Steam Release Valve is in "Seal" (closed) position. Press START/STOP.

2. Once cooking is complete, natural release pressure 5 minutes. Release remaining pressure. Divide mixture evenly among eight serving bowls. Top with cherries and oranges.

4 **cups water**

2 **cups old-fashioned oats**

¼ **cup sugar**

2 **tablespoons unsweetened cocoa powder**

2 **cups fresh pitted cherries or frozen dark sweet cherries**

2 **cans (11 ounces *each*) mandarin orange segments in light syrup, rinsed and drained**

1. Combine water, oats, sugar and cocoa in **CROCK-POT®** Express Crock Multi-Cooker; stir to blend. Secure lid. Press SLOW COOK, set temperature to LOW and time to 8 hours. Make sure Steam Release Valve is in the "Release" (open) position. Press START/STOP.

2. Once cooking is complete, divide mixture evenly among eight serving bowls. Top with cherries and oranges.

PUMPKIN CUSTARD

MAKES 6 SERVINGS

1 **cup canned solid-pack pumpkin**

1/2 **cup packed brown sugar**

2 **eggs, beaten**

1/2 **teaspoon ground ginger**

1/2 **teaspoon grated lemon peel**

1/2 **teaspoon ground cinnamon, plus additional for garnish**

1 **can (12 ounces) evaporated milk**

2 **cups water**

1. Combine pumpkin, brown sugar, eggs, ginger, lemon peel and 1/2 teaspoon cinnamon in large bowl; stir in evaporated milk. Divide mixture among six (6-ounce) ramekins or custard cups. Cover each cup tightly with foil.

2. Pour water into **CROCK-POT®** Express Crock Multi-Cooker. Place rack in Express Crock; stack ramekins on rack. Secure lid. Press STEAM, set pressure to LOW and time to 10 minutes. Make sure Steam Release Valve is in the "Seal" (closed) position. Press START/STOP.

3. Once cooking is complete, natural release pressure 10 minutes. Release remaining pressure. Use rubber-tipped tongs or slotted spoon to remove ramekins from Express Crock. Sprinkle with additional ground cinnamon. Serve warm.

1 **cup canned solid-pack pumpkin**

1/2 **cup packed brown sugar**

2 **eggs, beaten**

1/2 **teaspoon ground ginger**

1/2 **teaspoon grated lemon peel**

1/2 **teaspoon ground cinnamon, plus additional for garnish**

1 **can (12 ounces) evaporated milk**

2 **cups water**

1. Combine pumpkin, brown sugar, eggs, ginger, lemon peel and 1/2 teaspoon cinnamon in large bowl; stir in evaporated milk. Divide mixture among six (6-ounce) ramekins or custard cups. Cover each cup tightly with foil.

2. Pour water into **CROCK-POT®** Express Crock Multi-Cooker. Place rack in Express Crock; stack ramekins on rack. Secure lid. Press SLOW COOK, set temperature to LOW and time to 4 hours. Make sure Steam Release Valve is in the "Release" (open) position. Press START/STOP.

3. Once cooking is complete, use rubber-tipped tongs or slotted spoon to remove ramekins from Express Crock. Sprinkle with additional ground cinnamon. Serve warm.

PEAR CRUNCH

MAKES 4 SERVINGS

FAST

1 can (8 ounces) crushed pineapple in juice, undrained

¼ cup pineapple or apple juice

3 tablespoons dried cranberries

1½ teaspoons quick-cooking tapioca

¼ teaspoon vanilla

2 pears, cored and halved

¼ cup granola with almonds

Sprigs fresh mint (optional)

1. Combine pineapple, pineapple juice, cranberries, tapioca and vanilla in **CROCK-POT®** Express Crock Multi-Cooker; stir to blend. Top with pears, cut sides down. Secure lid. Press DESSERT, set pressure to HIGH and time to 5 minutes. Make sure Steam Release Valve is in the "Seal" (closed) position. Press START/STOP.

2. Once cooking is complete, quick release pressure. Arrange pear halves on serving plates. Spoon pineapple mixture over pear halves. Sprinkle with granola. Garnish with mint.

SLOW

1 can (8 ounces) crushed pineapple in juice, undrained

¼ cup pineapple or apple juice

3 tablespoons dried cranberries

1½ teaspoons quick-cooking tapioca

¼ teaspoon vanilla

2 pears, cored and halved

¼ cup granola with almonds

Sprigs fresh mint (optional)

1. Combine pineapple, pineapple juice, cranberries, tapioca and vanilla in **CROCK-POT®** Express Crock Multi-Cooker; stir to blend. Top with pears, cut sides down. Secure lid. Press SLOW COOK, set temperature to LOW and time to 3½ to 4 hours. Make sure Steam Release Valve is in the "Release" (open) position. Press START/STOP.

2. Once cooking is complete, arrange pear halves on serving plates. Spoon pineapple mixture over pear halves. Sprinkle with granola. Garnish with mint.

VANILLA SOUR CREAM CHEESECAKE

MAKES 6 TO 8 SERVINGS

FAST

¾ cup graham cracker crumbs

¼ cup plus 3 tablespoons sugar, divided

¼ teaspoon ground nutmeg

2 tablespoons unsalted butter, melted

1 package (8 ounces) cream cheese, softened

2 eggs

¼ cup sour cream

1½ teaspoons vanilla

1½ tablespoons all-purpose flour

2 cups water

Fresh strawberries, sliced (optional)

Sprigs fresh mint (optional)

1. Cut parchment paper to fit bottom of 7-inch springform pan that fits inside of **CROCK-POT®** Express Crock Multi-Cooker. Lightly spray bottom and side of pan with nonstick cooking spray. Wrap bottom and side of pan with foil. Prepare foil handles (page 13).

2. Combine graham cracker crumbs, 1 tablespoon sugar and nutmeg in medium bowl; stir to blend. Stir in butter until well blended. Press mixture into bottom and 1 inch up sides of prepared pan. Freeze 10 minutes.

3. Meanwhile, beat cream cheese in large bowl with electric mixer at high speed 3 to 4 minutes or until smooth. Add remaining ¼ cup plus 2 tablespoons sugar; beat 1 to 2 minutes. Beat in eggs, sour cream and vanilla until blended. Stir in flour. Pour batter into crust. Cover pan tightly with foil.

4. Place rack in Express Crock; add water. Place prepared pan on rack using foil handles. Secure lid. Press DESSERT, set pressure to HIGH and time to 40 minutes. Make sure Steam Release Valve is in the "Seal" (closed) position. Press START/STOP.

5. Once cooking is complete, quick release pressure. Remove pan from Express Crock to wire rack using foil handles. Cool 1 hour. Run thin knife around edge of cheesecake to loosen (do not remove side of pan). Refrigerate 2 to 3 hours or overnight.

6. Remove side and bottom of pan; remove cheesecake to serving plate. Cut into wedges to serve. Top with strawberries, if desired. Garnish with mint.

SLOW

¾ cup graham cracker crumbs

¼ cup plus 3 tablespoons sugar, divided

¼ teaspoon ground nutmeg

2 tablespoons unsalted butter, melted

1 package (8 ounces) cream cheese, softened

2 eggs

¼ cup sour cream

1½ teaspoons vanilla

1½ tablespoons all-purpose flour

2 cups water

Fresh strawberries, sliced (optional)

Sprigs fresh mint (optional)

1. Cut parchment paper to fit bottom of 7-inch springform pan that fits inside of **CROCK-POT®** Express Crock Multi-Cooker. Lightly spray bottom and side of pan with nonstick cooking spray. Wrap bottom and side of pan with foil. Prepare foil handles (page 13).

2. Combine graham cracker crumbs, 1 tablespoon sugar and nutmeg in medium bowl; stir to blend. Stir in butter until well blended. Press mixture into bottom and 1 inch up sides of prepared pan. Freeze 10 minutes.

3. Meanwhile, beat cream cheese in large bowl with electric mixer at high speed 3 to 4 minutes or until smooth. Add remaining 1/4 cup plus 2 tablespoons sugar; beat 1 to 2 minutes. Beat in eggs, sour cream and vanilla until blended. Stir in flour. Pour batter into crust. Cover pan tightly with foil.

4. Place rack in Express Crock; add water. Place prepared pan on rack using foil handles. Secure lid. Press SLOW COOK, set temperature to HIGH and time to 2 hours. Make sure Steam Release Valve is in the "Release" (open) position. Press START/STOP.

5. Once cooking is complete, remove pan from Express Crock to wire rack using foil handles. Cool 1 hour. Run thin knife around edge of cheesecake to loosen (do not remove side of pan). Refrigerate 2 to 3 hours or overnight.

6. Remove side and bottom of pan; remove cheesecake to serving plate. Cut into wedges to serve. Top with strawberries, if desired. Garnish with mint.

CHERRY RICE PUDDING

MAKES 6 SERVINGS

FAST

2 cups water

1 cup uncooked long grain rice

1/4 teaspoon salt

1 1/2 cups milk

3 eggs

1/2 cup sugar

1/4 cup dried cherries or cranberries

1/2 teaspoon almond extract

Ground nutmeg (optional)

1. Combine water, rice and salt in **CROCK-POT®** Express Crock Multi-Cooker; stir to blend. Secure lid. Press RICE/RISOTTO, set pressure to HIGH and time to 6 minutes. Make sure Steam Release Valve is in the "Seal" (closed) position. Press START/STOP.

2. Once cooking is complete, natural release pressure 10 minutes. Release remaining pressure. Whisk milk, eggs, sugar, cherries and almond extract in small bowl until blended. Press BROWN/SAUTÉ on Express Crock. Stir milk mixture into cooked rice; cook, uncovered, on HIGH 1 minute. Immediately remove pudding to serving bowls. Let stand 15 minutes. Garnish with nutmeg.

SLOW

1 1/2 cups milk

1 cup hot cooked rice

3 eggs, beaten

1/2 cup sugar

1/4 cup dried cherries or cranberries

1/2 teaspoon almond extract

1/4 teaspoon salt

Ground nutmeg (optional)

1. Combine milk, rice, eggs, sugar, cherries, almond extract and salt in **CROCK-POT®** Express Crock Multi-Cooker; stir to blend. Secure lid. Press SLOW COOK, set temperature to LOW and time to 4 to 5 hours. Make sure Steam Release Valve is in the "Release" (open) position. Press START/STOP.

2. Once cooking is complete, remove pudding to serving bowls. Let stand 15 minutes. Garnish with nutmeg.

CINNAMON-GINGER POACHED PEARS

MAKES 6 SERVINGS

FAST

3 cups water	2 whole cinnamon sticks	6 Bosc or Anjou pears, peeled and cored
1 cup sugar	1 tablespoon chopped candied ginger	
10 slices (¼ inch thick) fresh ginger		

1. Combine water, sugar, fresh ginger, cinnamon and candied ginger in **CROCK-POT®** Express Crock Multi-Cooker. Add rack; place pears on top. Secure lid. Press STEAM, set pressure to LOW and time to 3 minutes. Make sure Steam Release Valve is in the "Seal" (closed) position. Press START/STOP.

2. Once cooking is complete, quick release pressure. Remove pears to large serving platter. Press BROWN/SAUTÉ on Express Crock; cook syrup, uncovered, on HIGH 10 minutes or until thickened. Remove and discard cinnamon sticks. Drizzle pears with syrup to serve.

SLOW

3 cups water	2 whole cinnamon sticks	6 Bosc or Anjou pears, peeled and cored
1 cup sugar	1 tablespoon chopped candied ginger	
10 slices (¼ inch thick) fresh ginger		

1. Combine water, sugar, ginger, cinnamon and candied ginger in **CROCK-POT®** Express Crock Multi-Cooker. Add rack; place pears on top. Secure lid. Press SLOW COOK, set temperature and time to LOW 4 to 6 hours or to HIGH 1½ to 2 hours. Make sure Steam Release Valve is in the "Release" (open) position. Press START/STOP.

2. Once cooking is complete, remove pears to large serving platter. Press BROWN/SAUTÉ on Express Crock; cook syrup, uncovered, on HIGH 10 minutes or until thickened. Remove and discard cinnamon sticks. Drizzle pears with syrup to serve.

CHOCOLATE CHIP BREAD PUDDING

MAKES 4 SERVINGS

FAST

Butter, softened

1½ **cups water**

3 **slices (¾-inch-thick) day-old challah***

4 **tablespoons semisweet chocolate chips**

3 **eggs**

1½ **cups half-and-half**

⅓ **cup granulated sugar**

½ **teaspoon vanilla**

⅛ **teaspoon salt**

Powdered sugar

Fresh fruit (optional)

*Challah is usually braided. If you use brioche or another rich egg bread, slice bread to fit soufflé dish or round baking dish.

1. Butter 6- to 7-inch (1½-quart) soufflé dish or round baking dish that fits inside of **CROCK-POT®** Express Crock Multi-Cooker. Prepare foil handles (page 13). Place rack in Express Crock; add water. Arrange 1½ bread slices in bottom of prepared dish. Sprinkle with 2 tablespoons chocolate chips. Repeat layers with remaining bread and chocolate chips.

2. Beat eggs in medium bowl. Add half-and-half, granulated sugar, vanilla and salt; stir to blend. Pour egg mixture over bread layers. Press bread into liquid. Set aside 10 minutes or until liquid is absorbed. Cover dish with buttered foil, buttered side down.

3. Place prepared dish on rack using foil handles. Secure lid. Press DESSERT, set pressure to HIGH and time to 45 minutes. Make sure Steam Release Valve is in the "Seal" (closed) position. Press START/STOP.

4. Once cooking is complete, natural release pressure 10 minutes. Release remaining pressure. Remove dish using foil handles. Let stand 10 minutes. Sprinkle with powdered sugar. Garnish with fruit.

SLOW

Butter, softened

1½ **cups water**

3 **slices (¾-inch-thick) day-old challah***

4 **tablespoons semisweet chocolate chips**

3 **eggs**

1½ **cups half-and-half**

⅓ **cup granulated sugar**

½ **teaspoon vanilla**

⅛ **teaspoon salt**

Powdered sugar

Fresh fruit (optional)

*Challah is usually braided. If you use brioche or another rich egg bread, slice bread to fit soufflé dish or round baking dish.

1. Butter 6- to 7-inch (1½-quart) soufflé dish or round baking dish that fits inside of **CROCK-POT®** Express Crock Multi-Cooker. Prepare foil handles (page 13). Place rack in Express Crock; add water. Arrange 1½ bread slices in bottom of dish. Sprinkle with 2 tablespoons chocolate chips. Repeat layers with remaining bread and chocolate chips.

2. Beat eggs in medium bowl. Add half-and-half, granulated sugar, vanilla and salt; stir to blend. Pour egg mixture over bread layers. Press bread into liquid. Set aside 10 minutes or until liquid is absorbed. Cover dish with buttered foil, buttered side down.

3. Place prepared baking dish on rack using foil handles. Secure lid. Press SLOW COOK, set temperature to HIGH and time to 3 hours. Make sure Steam Release Valve is in the "Release" (open) position. Press START/STOP.

4. Once cooking is complete, remove dish using foil handles. Let stand 10 minutes. Sprinkle with powdered sugar. Garnish with fruit.

CHERRY DELIGHT

MAKES 8 TO 10 SERVINGS

FAST

1½ cups water
1 can (21 ounces) cherry pie filling

1 package (about 18 ounces) yellow cake mix
½ cup (1 stick) butter, melted

⅓ cup chopped walnuts

1. Spray 6- to 7-inch (1½-quart) soufflé dish or round baking dish that fits inside of **CROCK-POT®** Express Crock Multi-Cooker with nonstick cooking spray. Prepare foil handles (page 13). Place rack in Express Crock; add water.

2. Add pie filling to prepared dish. Combine cake mix and butter in medium bowl; spread evenly over pie filling. Cover dish with foil; place in Express Crock, using foil handles. Secure lid. Press DESSERT, set pressure to LOW and time to 10 minutes. Make sure Steam Release Valve is in the "Seal" (closed) position. Press START/STOP.

3. Once cooking is complete, quick release pressure. Remove dish using foil handles. Sprinkle with walnuts.

SLOW

1½ cups water
1 can (21 ounces) cherry pie filling

1 package (about 18 ounces) yellow cake mix
½ cup (1 stick) butter, melted

⅓ cup chopped walnuts

1. Spray 6- to 7-inch (1½-quart) soufflé dish or round baking dish that fits inside of **CROCK-POT®** Express Crock Multi-Cooker with nonstick cooking spray. Prepare foil handles (page 13). Place rack in Express Crock; add water.

2. Add pie filling to prepared dish. Combine cake mix and butter in medium bowl; spread evenly over pie filling. Cover dish with foil; place in Express Crock using foil handles. Secure lid. Press SLOW COOK, set temperature and time to LOW 3 to 4 hours or to HIGH 1½ to 2 hours. Make sure Steam Release Valve is in the "Release" (open) position. Press START/STOP.

3. Once cooking is complete, remove dish using foil handles. Sprinkle with walnuts.

BROWNIE BOTTOMS

MAKES 6 SERVINGS

FAST

2 cups water, divided

2½ cups packaged brownie mix

1 package (2¾ ounces) instant chocolate pudding mix

½ cup milk chocolate chips

2 eggs, beaten

3 tablespoons butter, melted

½ cup packed brown sugar

2 tablespoons unsweetened cocoa powder

Whipped cream or ice cream (optional)

1. Spray 6- or 7-inch (1½-quart) soufflé dish or round baking dish that fits inside of **CROCK-POT®** Express Crock Multi-Cooker with nonstick cooking spray. Prepare foil handles (page 13). Place rack and 1½ cups water in Express Crock.

2. Combine brownie mix, pudding mix, chocolate chips, eggs and butter in large bowl; stir until well blended. Combine brown sugar, remaining ½ cup water and cocoa in medium microwavable bowl. Microwave on HIGH 1 minute. Pour boiling sugar mixture over batter. Cover dish with foil; place in Express Crock using foil handles. Secure lid. Press DESSERT, set pressure to HIGH and time to 30 minutes. Make sure Steam Release Valve is in the "Seal" (closed) position. Press START/STOP.

3. Once cooking is complete, quick release pressure. Remove dish using foil handles. Let stand 10 minutes. Serve with whipped cream, if desired.

SLOW

2 cups water, divided

2½ cups packaged brownie mix

1 package (2¾ ounces) instant chocolate pudding mix

½ cup milk chocolate chips

2 eggs, beaten

3 tablespoons butter, melted

½ cup packed brown sugar

2 tablespoons unsweetened cocoa powder

Whipped cream or ice cream (optional)

1. Spray 6- or 7-inch (1½-quart) soufflé dish or round baking dish that fits inside of **CROCK-POT®** Express Crock Multi-Cooker with nonstick cooking spray. Prepare foil handles (page 13). Place rack and 1½ cups water in Express Crock.

2. Combine brownie mix, pudding mix, chocolate chips, eggs and butter in large bowl; stir until well blended. Combine brown sugar, remaining ½ cup water and cocoa in medium microwavable bowl. Microwave on HIGH 1 minute. Pour boiling sugar mixture over batter. Cover dish with foil; place in Express Crock using foil handles. Secure lid. Press SLOW COOK, set temperature to HIGH and time to 1½ hours. Make sure Steam Release Valve is in the "Release" (open) position. Press START/STOP.

3. Once cooking is complete, remove dish using foil handles. Let stand 10 minutes. Serve with whipped cream, if desired.

CRAN-CHERRY BREAD PUDDING

MAKES 12 SERVINGS

1½ cups water

¾ cup whipping cream

2 egg yolks, beaten

3 tablespoons sugar

⅛ teaspoon kosher salt

¾ teaspoon cherry extract

⅓ cup dried sweetened cranberries

⅓ cup golden raisins

¼ cup whole candied red cherries, halved

¼ cup dry sherry

3 cups unseasoned stuffing mix

½ cup white chocolate baking chips

Whipped cream (optional)

1. Spray 6- to 7-inch (1½-quart) soufflé dish or round baking dish that fits inside of **CROCK-POT®** Express Crock Multi-Cooker with nonstick cooking spray. Prepare foil handles (page 13). Place rack in Express Crock; add water.

2. Press BROWN/SAUTÉ on Express Crock. Add cream, egg yolks, sugar and salt; cook and stir on HIGH 5 minutes or until mixture coats back of spoon. Remove Express Crock to large bowl of ice water; stir to cool. Stir in cherry extract. Remove to separate large bowl; press plastic wrap onto surface of custard. Refrigerate.

3. Combine cranberries, raisins and cherries in small bowl. Press BROWN/SAUTÉ on Express Crock; heat sherry, uncovered, on HIGH until warm. Pour over fruit; let stand 10 minutes. Wipe Express Crock clean.

4. Fold stuffing mix and baking chips into custard. Drain fruit, reserving sherry; stir into custard. Pour into prepared dish. Top with reserved sherry; cover tightly with foil. Place dish on rack using foil handles. Secure lid. Press DESSERT, set pressure to HIGH and time to 45 minutes. Make sure Steam Release Valve is in the "Seal" (closed) position. Press START/STOP.

5. Once cooking is complete, natural release pressure 10 minutes. Release remaining pressure. Remove dish using foil handles. Uncover; let stand 10 minutes. Serve warm with whipped cream, if desired.

1½ cups water

¼ cup whipping cream

2 egg yolks, beaten

3 tablespoons sugar

⅛ teaspoon kosher salt

¾ teaspoon cherry extract

⅓ cup dried sweetened cranberries

⅓ cup golden raisins

¼ cup whole candied red cherries, halved

¼ cup dry sherry

3 cups unseasoned stuffing mix

½ cup white chocolate baking chips

Whipped cream (optional)

1. Spray 6- to 7-inch (1½-quart) soufflé dish or round baking dish that fits inside of **CROCK-POT®** Express Crock Multi-Cooker with nonstick cooking spray. Prepare foil handles (page 13). Place rack in Express Crock; add water.

2. Press BROWN/SAUTÉ on Express Crock. Add cream, egg yolks, sugar and salt; cook and stir on HIGH 5 minutes or until mixture coats back of spoon. Remove Express Crock to large bowl of ice water; stir to cool. Stir in cherry extract. Remove to separate large bowl; press plastic wrap onto surface of custard. Refrigerate.

3. Combine cranberries, raisins and cherries in small bowl. Press BROWN/SAUTÉ on Express Crock; heat sherry, uncovered, on HIGH until warm. Pour over fruit; let stand 10 minutes. Wipe Express Crock clean.

4. Fold stuffing mix and baking chips into custard. Drain fruit, reserving sherry; stir into custard. Pour into prepared dish. Top with reserved sherry; cover tightly with foil. Place dish on rack using foil handles. Secure lid. Press SLOW COOK, set temperature to LOW and time to 4 to 5 hours. Make sure Steam Release Valve is in the "Release" (open) position. Press START/STOP.

5. Once cooking is complete and pudding springs back when touched, remove dish using foil handles to wire rack. Uncover; let stand 10 minutes. Serve warm with whipped cream, if desired.

OATMEAL CRÈME BRÛLÉE

MAKES 4 TO 6 SERVINGS

1½ cups water

6 egg yolks

½ cup granulated sugar

½ teaspoon salt

2 cups whipping cream

1 teaspoon vanilla

3 cups quick-cooking oats

¼ cup packed light brown sugar

Fresh berries (optional)

1. Spray 6- to 7-inch (1½-quart) soufflé dish or round baking dish that fits inside of **CROCK-POT®** Express Crock Multi-Cooker with nonstick cooking spray. Place rack in Express Crock; add water. Prepare foil handles (page 13).

2. Whisk egg yolks, granulated sugar and salt in medium bowl until blended. Add cream and vanilla; whisk until blended. Stir in oats; pour into prepared dish. Cover with foil. Place in Express Crock using foil handles. Secure lid. Press DESSERT, set pressure to HIGH and time to 40 minutes. Make sure Steam Release Valve is in "Seal" (closed) position. Press START/STOP.

3. Once cooking is complete, quick release pressure. Remove dish from Express Crock using foil handles. Sprinkle brown sugar over surface of custard. If desired, place under broiler 3 to 5 minutes to melt brown sugar. Serve with berries, if desired.

1½ cups water

6 egg yolks

½ cup granulated sugar

½ teaspoon salt

2 cups whipping cream

1 teaspoon vanilla

3 cups quick-cooking oats

¼ cup packed light brown sugar

Fresh berries (optional)

1. Spray 6- to 7-inch (1½-quart) soufflé dish or round baking dish that fits inside of **CROCK-POT®** Express Crock Multi-Cooker with nonstick cooking spray. Place rack in Express Crock; add water. Prepare foil handles (page 13).

2. Whisk egg yolks, granulated sugar and salt in medium bowl until blended. Add cream and vanilla; whisk until blended. Stir in oats; pour into prepared dish. Cover with foil. Place in Express Crock using foil handles. Secure lid. Press SLOW COOK, set temperature to LOW and time to 3 to 3½ hours. Make sure Steam Release Valve is in the "Release" (open) position. Press START/STOP.

3. Once cooking is complete and custard is set, remove dish from Express Crock using foil handles. Sprinkle brown sugar over surface of custard. If desired, place under broiler 3 to 5 minutes to melt brown sugar. Serve with berries, if desired.

FRENCH TOAST BREAD PUDDING

MAKES 6 TO 8 SERVINGS

FAST

1 cup water	2 eggs	1/8 teaspoon ground nutmeg
1 tablespoon packed dark brown sugar	1 cup whipping cream	Whipped cream (optional)
1 teaspoon ground cinnamon	1 cup half-and-half	*If unavailable, cut day-old 24-ounce loaf of white sandwich bread into 1-inch-thick slices.*
8 ounces French bread baguette, sliced 1-inch thick and halved (2-inch pieces)	1/2 cup plus 2 tablespoons granulated sugar	
	1 teaspoon vanilla	
	1/8 teaspoon salt	

1. Spray 6- to 7-inch (1½-quart) soufflé dish or round baking dish that fits inside of **CROCK-POT®** Express Crock Multi-Cooker with nonstick cooking spray. Prepare foil handles (page 13). Place rack in Express Crock; add water. Combine brown sugar and cinnamon in small bowl; stir to blend. Reserve 1 tablespoon; set aside.

2. Arrange bread slices in single layer in prepared dish. Sprinkle half of remaining cinnamon mixture over bread. Repeat layers with remaining bread and cinnamon mixture.

3. Beat eggs in medium bowl. Add cream, half-and-half, granulated sugar, vanilla, salt and nutmeg. Pour cream mixture over bread; press bread down lightly. Set aside 10 minutes or until liquid is absorbed. Sprinkle reserved cinnamon mixture on top. Cover dish with foil.

4. Place prepared dish on rack using foil handles. Secure lid. Press DESSERT, set pressure to HIGH and time to 45 minutes. Make sure Steam Release Valve is in the "Seal" (closed) position. Press START/STOP.

5. Once cooking is complete, natural release pressure 8 minutes. Release remaining pressure. Remove dish using foil handles; let stand 10 minutes. Spoon into bowls; top with whipped cream, if desired.

SLOW

1 cup water	2 eggs	1/8 teaspoon ground nutmeg
1 tablespoon packed dark brown sugar	1 cup whipping cream	Whipped cream (optional)
1 teaspoon ground cinnamon	1 cup half-and-half	*If unavailable, cut day-old 24-ounce loaf of white sandwich bread into 1-inch-thick slices.*
8 ounces French bread baguette, sliced 1-inch thick and halved (2-inch pieces)	1/2 cup plus 2 tablespoons granulated sugar	
	1 teaspoon vanilla	
	1/4 teaspoon salt	

1. Spray 6- to 7-inch (1½-quart) soufflé dish or round baking dish that fits inside of **CROCK-POT®** Express Crock Multi-Cooker with nonstick cooking spray. Prepare foil handles (page 13). Place rack in Express Crock; add water. Combine brown sugar and cinnamon in small bowl; stir to blend. Reserve 1 tablespoon; set aside.

2. Arrange bread slices in single layer in prepared dish. Sprinkle half of remaining cinnamon mixture over bread. Repeat layers with remaining bread and cinnamon mixture.

3. Beat eggs in medium bowl. Add cream, half-and-half, granulated sugar, vanilla, salt and nutmeg. Pour cream mixture over bread; press bread down lightly. Set aside 10 minutes or until liquid is absorbed. Sprinkle reserved cinnamon mixture on top. Cover dish with foil.

4. Place prepared dish on rack using foil handles. Secure lid. Press SLOW COOK, set temperature and time to LOW 3 to 4 hours or to HIGH 1½ to 2 hours. Make sure Steam Release Valve is in the "Release" (open) position. Press START/STOP.

5. Once cooking is complete, remove dish using foil handles. Let stand 10 minutes. Spoon into bowls; top with whipped cream, if desired.

Chicken Ramen Noodle Bowls
(page 114)

INDEX

METRIC CONVERSION CHART

VOLUME MEASUREMENTS (dry)

1/8 teaspoon = 0.5 mL
1/4 teaspoon = 1 mL
1/2 teaspoon = 2 mL
3/4 teaspoon = 4 mL
1 teaspoon = 5 mL
1 tablespoon = 15 mL
2 tablespoons = 30 mL
1/4 cup = 60 mL
1/3 cup = 75 mL
1/2 cup = 125 mL
2/3 cup = 150 mL
3/4 cup = 175 mL
1 cup = 250 mL
2 cups = 1 pint = 500 mL
3 cups = 750 mL
4 cups = 1 quart = 1 L

VOLUME MEASUREMENTS (fluid)

1 fluid ounce (2 tablespoons) = 30 mL
4 fluid ounces (1/2 cup) = 125 mL
8 fluid ounces (1 cup) = 250 mL
12 fluid ounces (1 1/2 cups) = 375 mL
16 fluid ounces (2 cups) = 500 mL

WEIGHTS (mass)

1/2 ounce = 15 g
1 ounce = 30 g
3 ounces = 90 g
4 ounces = 120 g
8 ounces = 225 g
10 ounces = 285 g
12 ounces = 360 g
16 ounces = 1 pound = 450 g

DIMENSIONS

1/16 inch = 2 mm
1/8 inch = 3 mm
1/4 inch = 6 mm
1/2 inch = 1.5 cm
3/4 inch = 2 cm
1 inch = 2.5 cm

OVEN TEMPERATURES

250°F = 120°C
275°F = 140°C
300°F = 150°C
325°F = 160°C
350°F = 180°C
375°F = 190°C
400°F = 200°C
425°F = 220°C
450°F = 230°C

BAKING PAN SIZES

Utensil	Size in Inches/Quarts	Metric Volume	Size in Centimeters
Baking or	8×8×2	2 L	20×20×5
Cake Pan	9×9×2	2.5 L	23×23×5
(square or	12×8×2	3 L	30×20×5
rectangular)	13×9×2	3.5 L	33×23×5
Loaf Pan	8×4×3	1.5 L	20×10×7
	9×5×3	2 L	23×13×7
Round Layer	8×1½	1.2 L	20×4
Cake Pan	9×1½	1.5 L	23×4
Pie Plate	8×1¼	750 mL	20×3
	9×1¼	1 L	23×3
Baking Dish	1 quart	1 L	—
or Casserole	1½ quart	1.5 L	—
	2 quart	2 L	—